SUPER BRAIN:

MAXIMIZE YOUR BRAIN HEALTH
FOR A BETTER LIFE

WHAT OTHERS HAVE SAID

What a fantastic, straightforward and honest book. Congratulations, Dr. Jay Sordean!
Fabienne Slama, Author of <u>Renaissance Woman</u>

<u>Super Brain: Maximize Your Brain Health For A Better Life</u> cuts straight to the chase on what you need to do to make the most of the opportunities that come your way.
Alexander Robert Figueroa, Author of <u>Assess This</u>!

Dr. Jay's "B.R.A.I.N." Formula for brain health is absolutely helpful! What a fantastic book!
Jarod Anderson and T.L. Anderson, Authors of <u>Five Star Mentality</u>

A must-read for anyone who wants to have a supercharged brain.
Jeffrey Alan Grinel, Author of <u>Don't Rack Your Brain, RockUrBrain</u>

The information in this book just works. I knew there should be an easy way to work on your memory every day to create a vibrant life and this is it.
Rondea Wine, Author of <u>Stop The Junk</u>

Here is a powerhouse book of tips, tactics and approaches for our brain that simply work. A fantastic book.
Dr. Andrea Maxim, ND, Author of <u>MAXIMized Health</u>

Powerful, practical and solid advice on brain health. Apply Dr. Jay's knowledge and you'll feel much more control of your life.
Ahmad Duranai B. Arch., MBA, OAA, BTC, Author of <u>The Leadership Zone</u>

This is a very current and important book and topic for anyone concerned about their optimal, future mental health and functioning.
Byron B. Fong, DOM, LAc, Third Generation Chinese Medicine Doctor

SUPER BRAIN:
MAXIMIZE YOUR BRAIN HEALTH
FOR A BETTER LIFE

DR. JAY SORDEAN

BEST-SELLING AUTHOR & CLINICIAN
APPEARING ON
ABC, CBS, NBC, FOX, AND CW

ISBN-10: 1514734362 ISBN-13:978-1514734360
Library of Congress Control Number: 2015911638
CreateSpace Independent Publishing Platform,
North Charleston, SC

DISCLAIMER: The information written in this book is designed to provide helpful information on Alzheimer's, memory, and the subjects discussed. It is not comprehensive by any means. The book is not meant to diagnose or treat any medical condition, or to replace the advice of your physician(s). The author of this book does not claim to have found a cure for Alzheimer's or any other specific condition.

The reader should regularly consult a physician in matters related to his or her health, particularly with respect to any symptoms that may require diagnosis or medical attention. For diagnosis or treatment of any medical problem, consult your own physician(s).

The publisher and authors are not responsible or liable for any damages or negative consequences from any treatment, action, application or preparation to any person reading or following the information in this book. References are provide for informational purposes only and do not constitute endorsement of any websites or other sources. Readers should be aware that the websites listed in this book may change.

DISCLOSURE: Some of the links are to places that you can purchase products that the author recommends. The author or The Redwood Clinic may receive compensation or fees for your purchases – that covers the costs of business and publication expenses and in no way diminishes the value of the suggestions or recommendations.

DEDICATION

May this book serve as inspiration to many people, so that their lives are better and consequently the Earth becomes a more peaceful and harmonious place to live.

THANKS AND ACKNOWLEDGMENTS

The input, ideas, and support of many people made this book a reality. My thanks go out to those here now and those whose influence in the past continues with me today, including:

My Family Members, John Sordean, Hattie Sordean, Uncle Russ Lamb, Aunt Judy Lamb, Aunt Dottie Sordean, Andrea Mintzer, Judy Sordean, Eliot Mintzer, Sigal Gafni, Savyon Gafni Sordean, Elah Gafni Sordean, Cathy Frakes, Donna Geniti, Erelah Gafni, Layla Gafni Kubukeli, Randy Lamb, Priscilla Johnson, other family members on the Sordean, Bridgford, Lamb and Gafni lineages, including cousins, nieces, nephews, and once-removeds and grand- and great-grandparents.

Interviewees: Byron Fong LAc, Austin Hill Shaw, Joanny Liu OMD, Geoff Olsen, Joseph Smith DC, Michael Nelson MD, Rob Demartino DC, Kewesi Simon, Deborah Rozman PhD, Ben Bernstein PhD, Doug Kempton DC, Renee Dyer, Katinka Van dermerwe DC, Don Lawson, Cori Stern DC, Belinda Leung, Michael Gelbart PhD, Erica Shaver-Nelson, Marsha Peoples, Anne Sanabria, Shirley McElhatten, Micheal Pope PhD, David Blyweiss MD, Sergio Azzolino DC.

Other Resources: Aristo Vodjani PhD, Jeffrey S. Bland PhD, Colette Jones, Rick Huntoon DC, Marshal Mermel, Simon Gibson PT, Jeremy Smith, Jon Mazura MD.

People I have studied with or learned from in various ways: Michael E. Lara, MD, Paul Witcomb DC, Datis Kharrazian

DC, Martin Katz, Jared Kneebone, Michael Pearce DC, Dr. Dale Bredesen, Tony Robbins, John Assaraf, Benjamin Levy, Blair Singer, Richard Bandler, John Grinder, A.M. Krasner, Father Richard Mapplebeckpalmer, Frank Lamport, George Rodkey, Thom Hartmann, Mark Yuzuik, Simone Coulars, Joel Roberts, Roger Love, Cheri Tree, Lao Tzu, Chuang Tzu, The Dalai Lama, Miki Shima OMD, Matt VanBenschoten OMD, Yoshiaki Omura MD, Hidetaro Mori OMD, Black Card Books Publishing Staff, Marybeth Haines, Pam Grant Ryan, Celena Peet/Green Typewriter, Elizabeth Whipple, Nadine Samuels Photography, and many others.

<u>TV affiliates</u>: Clint Arthur and Alison Savitch, Adrienne Williams, Jennifer Schack, Izzy Karpinski, Alex Maragos, Adina Klein, Cory McPherrin, Kara Sewell, Jemelle Holopirek, Amanda Sanchez, Taylor Tucker, Raynard Gadson, Kristina Behr, JD Roberto, Cynthia Newell, Celina Tuason, Monica Jackson, Victoria Spilabotte, Tiffany Frowiss, Renee Kohn, Susan Hancock, John Carter, Holly Hendrick, Leslie Williams, Tom Crawford, Oprah, Mark Harmon, and others.

<u>Thousands of patients</u> I have had the pleasure and honor to work with over the last 30+ years. May I be able to help even better now through this book. <u>Friends and Acquaintances world-wide.</u> And <u>everyone who bought (and hopefully read) this book</u> and made it a bestseller.

Hand-drawn pictures by Simone Coulars. All other pictures and charts by Jay Sordean, rights obtained, or credited as noted.

CONTENTS

INTRODUCTION: WHY I AM INTERESTED IN THE BRAIN AND WHY I WROTE THIS BOOK

What is your most valuable asset? This is a key question to ask yourself in order to prioritize activities, actions, and how you spend your money - how you spend your life. We only have so many breaths, so many heartbeats, and so many moments in this lifetime. So it's good to pause and reassess your values occasionally.

When it comes to your body, I would suggest that your brain is your most valuable asset. There are other organs and limbs that you can live without, but your brain, followed by your heart, are the two primary organs necessary to have quality of life. So this is where I think and feel that one should start in prioritizing your health care time, energy, money, and attention. Why I have concluded that will become more evident throughout this book.

The age-old questions of who we truly are, what our personal value is, and where do thoughts and our self-awareness lie, are a wonderful place to start. However, I am not going to address these questions herein. There is not enough time in a lifetime to address even one of these questions adequately (even though they would be worthy and appropriate topics to include in a book about the brain and central nervous system in relationship to the whole body.)

Rather, let me share a personal story of how I came to become interested in the subject of maximizing the health of the brain to improve the quality of life.

Why I am Interested in the Brain, and Why I Wrote This Book

I was groomed, and even mentally programmed, to become a doctor from early childhood. My Uncle Russell, who was a highly skilled and respected medical doctor and general surgeon, told me from an early age that I was going to be a doctor like him.

My father, who worked as a white collar employee for Eli Lilly & Company for my entire life, had been a nurse in the Navy for several years around World War II. After leaving the Navy, he also studied to go to medical school and though he applied, he was not accepted.

Eventually he made a career working in packaging design and testing for Eli

Lilly & Company in Indianapolis, Indiana, my birth place. I felt like my father was disappointed that he hadn't been able to achieve his goal of being a physician, and many around him said that he would have been very good because of his attention to detail, ability to work with his hands and his warmth and patience. On the other hand, my mother said that my dad was actually happy with how his career turned out and that if he had been a doctor he would have had less time to spend with his family.

When I was thirteen or so I was walking through the bathroom off of our kitchen. That bathroom connected the kitchen to the master bedroom where my parents slept. As I passed by I saw my father was leaning over the sink, coughing, and the sink was filled with bright red blood. That turned out to be the start of the discovery and process of treating my father's lung cancer. Exactly why it occurred we don't know. He had been a smoker from an early age, as was the practice at that time. He especially smoked more when he was in the Navy, cigarettes being something that, I have been told, was readily available and cheaply provided to soldiers by the tobacco industry. He didn't smoke filtered cigarettes - they were the Chesterfield-, Pall Mall-, Lucky Strike-type cigarettes. They made my head spin when I smoked one and hadn't ever done so.

We did lots of family trips together to see other parts of the U.S. My father loved to travel and so would save up to take the family on trips to see national parks and other sights. A trip up to Mount Rushmore, the Grand Tetons, Yellowstone Park. Another to the Grand Canyon and California – Disneyland in Anaheim, San Diego where he had been stationed, and to Berkeley to see where all the Free Speech demonstrations had been going on. My mother loved to see universities, having been a teacher.

At any rate, on one of our trips up to visit friends in Michigan we children complained about the cigarette smoke in the car so much that my dad quit smoking cold turkey. We didn't even notice, and it hurt my father's feelings as my mother admonished us about later. It didn't seem to make a difference that he had quit smoking, he still got lung cancer.

Over the next 5 years my father was treated, in the late 60's and early 70's with the treatments available at the time as surgery was not an option. Radiation therapy in two different rounds years apart, causing a red burn on his chest that was surrounded by a purple tattooed target square.

In the last year of his life, my senior year in high school, he was not able to work. He was in the hospital for a short while and then returned home to finish his life out, confined to a bed largely in the final weeks as his body wasted away with no appetite. The last months when he was mobile he would say some very irrational things and was very stubborn about things like wanting to cut down a shrub in the front yard.

At the dinner table he would suddenly talk about something called "the safety factor" that didn't seem to fit the conversation. He also had to be watched carefully when we went to visit my older sister Judy at college because he would wonder off and not know how to find his way back. The cancer had spread to his brain and was causing his mental and cognitive functioning to weaken and become scrambled.

This experience of my father's change in personality and functioning due to brain dysregulation and damage is one of the reasons why I have always had an interest in the brain and how one can try to keep it healthy and enhance functioning.

CHAPTER 1: WHY YOU SHOULD CARE ABOUT YOUR BRAIN – YOUR MOST VALUABLE ASSET – AND WHY YOU SHOULD KNOW HOW YOUR NERVOUS SYSTEM WORKS.

Our Personal Experiences

We are our personal experiences. It has been said that there are three things that nobody can take from you: your experiences, what you have learned, and your memories. In actuality, if you don't have your memory function you lose your experiences and what you learned, at least at a conscious level.

So, when it comes down it, who we are are our own personal experiences. What family we are born into, the place or places we are born and brought up, what we are named and who raises us, this create the "Me" the "Who I am." When you go to sleep at night and wake up in the morning, if you say your name and describe who you are, it is your memory and experiences that define it. We are a composite of all we have done and learned, who we've met and where we've been. And how we feel about ourselves is strongly influenced by all those memories stored in our brain as well as the input we have at the moment.

Familial Influences

"Who I am" is a composition of many aspects. "Personality" is a component of "Who I am", my identity. Up-beat, intellectual, dominating, passive, intense, depressed - all are ways we might paint the picture of someone's personality. Sometimes we think of someone's personality as "They were just born that way." More of a genetic thing. Other times we attribute the personality traits to environmental factors - how we pattern after parents or role models, how we dress after fashion trends or if we rebel against the mainstream.

A woman growing up in Japan might have a quiet personality that is oriented around serving others. It is also possible that a thoughtless father treating her poorly and with disrespect will result in her turning out with an A typical personality. Instead of being a quiet and docile person, she will be independent, rebellious, and entrepreneurial. Either way, her personality is shaped by her experiences, and how those experiences are consolidated and reflected back out by the brain to body connection.

The relationships we create and grow up into are major determinants about so many things. I was moved to study medicine by the influence of my uncle, father, and even a grandfather. I acquired an ability, if my personality so moved me in the moment, to talk to total strangers in lines (Why in line is so much easier than locations?) because of my mother's influence and proclivities. My older boy cousin was a role model who I patterned after also in so many ways - enhancing my pleasure in building things, camping, and even shunning a career as a surgeon. Digging into your own past I'm sure that you will see behavioral traits you picked up from adults, parents, older siblings. People talk about that all the time, especially spouses talking about their parents' influences. That is, if they have parents. At any rate, the experiences we have influence who we are, and our brain is the recorder, re-order or, and conduit and conductor of our sometimes "Puppet like" behavior born of experiences.

External Sensory Input

Our brain is a sensory input interpreter and analyzer. Nerves pick up on information from inside and outside the body. The nerves connect into and with the brain. Our 5 primary senses are sight, hearing, smelling, tasting and touch. Each sensory avenue influences the brain in different areas and in different ways.

The auditory aspect of sensory understanding of the world can be divided into structured language and music. Each has different influences on the brain and our emotions and intelligence.

The voices we hear, with their emotional content, before birth, are those we are most influenced by at a deep survival level; this is because the survival brain, the brain stem functions, are most predominant at this stage of our development. Thus, when born, we are most attuned to our mother's and father's voices – or attuned to some other voices that we hear a lot.

Music also creates an influence on our brain function in utero and then later in life. Music has a certain structure, as do voices in a particular language. Learning new languages and listening to music, sometimes in deliberate combination, is a key way to improve brain health and the quality of our life. Listening to the sound of nature, when in nature, is also important to enhance brain clarity and efficiency.

The diversity of voices in music from pre-birth and into later life is a way to maximize brain function, innovation, and creativity, memory is also profoundly improved by this.

Languages

Learning 2 or more languages when young is shown to increase the ability of the brain to learn new things more easily. Learning several languages, even later in life also has brain maximizing effects that can also enhance one's work and money generating capabilities. In utero, the variety and diversity and sound environment your mother was in has significant influences on the survival brain. Easy and safe environment of the mother helps the child to start out with less stress responses, at least initially in life. If the mother is in dire straits, with insufficient nutrition and external survival issues, the child will start out life with more physiological, survival-based stress responses.

Over time an underlying anxiety, versus certainty, can be seen in the behavioral patterns. So trying to create a safer nutrition-rich pregnancy is certainly the ideal to enhance brain function. Of course, it doesn't mean that those born in very stressful environments can't overcome the deep-seated physiological stress responses hardwired more deeply in their nervous system. It just means that it needs to be discovered and recognized and remedial action taken as soon as possible. ASAP. Nerve cell plasticity is a flexible aspect and yet a rigidifying aspect too, which resists change.

Your Brain Generates Electrical Waves

Brain researchers have found that our brains emit electrical currents, also called brain waves, that can be measured in both strength and wave length. Light energies of different colors have different wave lengths, blue is shorter red is longer. Similarly, different states of physical consciousness have different corresponding dominant wave length and frequency ranges. They are simply labeled Alpha, Beta, Theta, Delta and Gamma but others have been elucidated as well. The wave lengths vary from less than 1 to 32 plus hertz (hertz is a measure of frequency). The first wave forms discovered were called Alpha. They were found from meditators, people praying, day dreaming, almost being asleep. A chart of the different wave frequencies are listed on the chart.

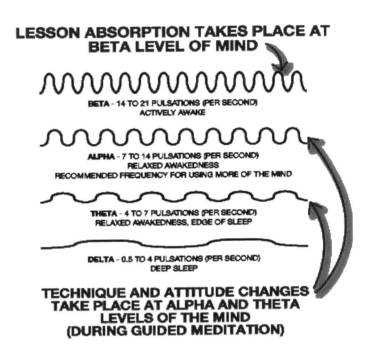

Chart of Brain Waves and correspondences with States of Mind

Age Predominant Brain Wave Patterns

It was discovered that in general the predominant wave frequency in a person's life is the one corresponding to their age during development. 12-24 hertz brain waves correspond to your brain's conscious faculties. Wave length of this type are more and more able to do more complicated tasks, and this brain wave pattern starts the maturation process predominantly from age 12 going to age 24. Thus, educational theory would design lessons bases on this cognitive ability, with education in various subjects introduced gradually so the nervous system is capable of meeting the task at hand.

The development of emotional responses also parallels this process. Although the correspondence of particular emotions and particular intellectual abilities is not exclusive to particular frequencies.
For example, learning several languages contiguously is probably easier in the earlier years of life than in later years. This is in spite of the general idea that the higher cortical wave length and functions of language are less dominant at an early age of human development. So exactly how emotions are linked to particular wave length ranges is not well understood. On the other hand, the brain stem emotions - survival emotions, are thought to be simpler and less subtle. Like hunger, pain, and sexual desire. These are lower frequency wave length-associated feelings (not to confuse them with lower level, or less important, feelings.)

Education and Success

Whether a child likes or hates education at an early age may influence their ability to maximize their brain function. Some education systems in schools are more rigid and regimented than others. If a child doesn't fit into the standard mold of educational development, that child might be considered distracted, a problem student, a disruptor of other students' learning, et cetera. That child might hate school and that can delay their ability to develop certain skills, like reading comprehension, until much later in life as an adult, or maybe not at all.

Mike McQueen, author of a book on how to get boys to read, has told me that this was the case for him. Oppositely, a 16 year old friend in Charleston, South Carolina quit school, studied on her own, and started college at age 15 prior to a car accident. The car accident made major memory difficulties although she made much faster recovery time from some physical limitations than anticipated by the use of acupuncture, massage, herbs, homeopathy, and mirror technologies thought to her by her neurologist.

As infants and toddlers we are just developing our verbal skills. When we are exposed to language environments, we learn the patterns of speech, hearing, and grammar necessary to communicate verbally with others around us. Our need to express our needs, desires, and observation drive us to try out these new sounds on others as soon as possible.

Typically, following just the sounds of crying, cooing, farting, and other hard to discern sounds of something, around age 1 to 2 our communication becomes clearer and understandable by those close to us and then by others. This process and ability follows and is dependent upon our brain changes as well as those of our vocal apparatus of lungs, larynx, tongue, mouth, jaws, et cetera.

The "Blank Slate"

At our earliest and most formative years the sensation impressions from the outside world are imprinting upon a fairly untainted and open slate. The memories we layer on our developing nervous system and general body form a foundation for how we operate in the world for the rest of our life; just like an operating system of a computer, the underlying matrix of our nervous system that starts with basic survival skills like eating, sleeping, walking, moving and digesting. Built on top of that is layered language, math, special, auditory, and kinesthetic and (feeling) differentiation skills. Memorization of certain songs, poems, rhymes and rhythms begin here and thus this is great time to teach children fundamental memory patterns, such as the alphabet if speaking English or the languages with an alphabet - like written structure and basic math facts like addition, subtraction, multiplication, and the division facts. The progression from more simple to more complex in education is based on understanding the developing and progressing ability of children to learn and remember.

Childhood experiences are varied anew. Every moment is unique and time seems to last forever. All of the sounds, sites, feelings, and emotions with taste and smell stimulate all parts of our body and nervous system. Having a broad availability of experiences creates a whole brain activation that sets us up for the ability to see details and get the big picture perspective in later years. This early life diffuse spreading of related sensations to parts of the brain and body - all related to particular and unique experiences - results in an integration of different parts of the body and brain. This integration helps us in later life to recall and access information under stress that may have been the difference between life and death. Promoting such integrative experiences early on puts a child on the fast track to success in the future.

Problem Solving

Problem solving is a fundamental skill set that each of us have intrinsically and also develops over time. As children we constantly have to figure out how to do new things. Sometimes on our own and sometimes with the help of others. Being engaged in the process of problem solving stimulates many parts of the brain. Sensory and muscle/motor nerve activity. Children getting lots of this type of varied stimulation develop innovative skills and are more creative in solving problems in the future as adults.

All parts of the body are involved in this process and the amount of new stimulation occurring overloads the memory processes of the brain. Thus, conscious readable or reliable memory is diminished while unconscious pattern traits are laid down for survival purposes. Thus, patterned sensory/motor tracks are the foundation for higher and more complex activities carried out as adults like complex sports and manual skills. The fun experience during these simple activities leads to fun in the future. Frustration overcome by persistence as a child often leads to perseverance in complex and perplexing tasks as an adult.

Proper nutrition and low sugar is a key element here.

While this integration of sensory and motor input occurs in the context of individual activity and emotions, the involvement of other humans or animals is a key ingredient that assist in innovation. Why might this be? The feeling of inseparability of oneself from the outside world, the world beyond our skin, is intrinsic at birth. The reality of inseparability never really leaves us as it is a fundamental fact of human and earthly life. While we may develop a sense of "Me versus other" as we age and are educated in various cultural settings, it is an artifact of culture when it results in individual recognition for achievement in life.

No one is born in and of themselves, no one spontaneously creates one's own food and sustenance, and no one creates or invents a totally new language or innovation. In spite of societal recognition in the form of patterns and individual recognition of words. Who would be there to create the recognition of the individual? Individual effort and neural patterns and emotional responses are a collective phenomenon. It is well that "Each" of us remembers that on a daily basis.

Locking our experiences into our brain over the course of our life starts out an organic process. We are born just taking in what we take in life. But humans have discovered more sophisticated and effective ways to capture our experiences so they last and can be shared with others and remembered for reflection and learning. Telling the story of what we've been through to the others is the basis of storytelling, sharing, and the building of myth, legend and culture. Verbal recitation pre-dates written language and our brains and bodies are well designed for this behavior.

Written Language

When the stories got too long or were repeated too often so as to become boring, or there were too many stories, or for other reasons -- people started creating a written system to convey or notate the stories and other experiences they found important for life, fun, feelings, and survival. Over centuries or millennia, the written symbols became complex enough to record things in detail. Thus, the experiences could be passed on. And it is our duty to do this type of writing to preserve our brain function for our future years.

As a natural outgrowth of sharing our experiences verbally to others and writing them down, internal reflections occurs without effort. In fact, we can't avoid internal reflection because that is actually the source of our ability to share verbally and write down our experiences. Of course, we start as children repeating what we heard from our parents, grandparents, siblings, friends, et cetera. Perhaps by rote, other times with our twist on it. But soon enough, whether as faithful transcription or fanciful fiction (if not flat out lying.) And then this can become an internal dialogue or monologue - unspoken and yet spoken inside our heads.

This is the question we may wonder "What is going on inside their heads?" when we encounter a silent person, a person who doesn't speak our language, someone who sleep, or someone apparently awake and yet labeled with dementia.

Why do we want to memorialize and pass on the experience and wisdom of others? Writing biographies of others is a common and very helpful method. I remember scouring the blue covered book section in my elementary school library for the biographies of "Famous" people from American history. Getting lost in those stories took me into worlds and times I would never encounter on my own.

> "I think literature creates reality or it is not literature at all."
> Carlos Fuentes.

The study of geographic locations and their features is something we each learn naturally. It is a survival mechanism as a child to find our way home.

And as a civilization or even a small community we have to know the details, features, natural features and other facts about where we live in order to survive and support future generations if that is something we actually desire. This can involve plants, water sources, roads, housing, and shelter and physical topographic features of where we live or travel.

Our personal and family survival and happiness depends on various tasks we must want to do. Preparing food, gather food, building things, driving a bike, car, donkey, cart, truck, train or plane; playing pianos, guitars, zithers, kotos, drums, bongos, trombones; play sports or card games; healing the sick; making movies; making things; all these are the products of some human activity. To perpetuate their existence for ourselves and others, we or someone has to pre-practice the detailed process of doing or making them and pass that onto others in some fashion. This might be apprenticeship, large classes, or even sometimes the training can be as simple as an outline how to do video.

What value does our experience have?

We all have experiences and resources that can benefit others. Monetizing (or making money from them) these requires efforts of some sorts. Connecting with others is a key element for making money off our experience and skills. We have to make the effort to meet and communicate effectively with others in order to have the opportunity to sell them on what we have to offer to them or others they know.

Just talking is not enough. Demonstrating how something is done is crucial in passing on the experience and ability to replicate. For example, teaching someone to dance by simply writing it on a piece of paper is not usually sufficient to create a good dancer. Actually showing the dance student, in person, exactly how the moves go, the rhythm, the pace, the subtle foot, hand and arm motions are key. In the case of driving a car, a personal instructor is necessary to not only teach a novice how to drive, but also to evaluate whether this person should be on the road after some practice. Learning to drive from a book alone is nearly impossible.

If we want to learn how to do tasks and jobs, it requires effective communication of many details to do a job or task effectively. By effectively dealing with a problem a client is having, the value of that solved problem is evident and payment can be made. Hence, using our various communication skills - visual, auditory, and kinesthetic - all are employed to achieve the desired outcome.

When we can effectively communicate what we can do to help someone else, the wheels of commerce, helping relationships, and healthy family dynamics are the results. Using our brain to the highest level of capability leads to a better life.

To fulfill our highest purpose we engage others in the task at hand to get there and to enjoy the journey along the way. To engage and train others, we must personally and completely understand and reflect upon the skills needed. Next we must systematize the skill--in other words, create a step-by-step process to the degree possible, to train someone else.

Lastly and equally important is to emotionally encourage others to achieve mastery of the skills we want to delegate to others. This is how we turn our job skills into training others effectively and thus leveraging our time.

Legacy Transmission

We want to pass on a legacy to family and friends and we do that through training others in the skills and ideas we've developed over the years. Some or all of those may have been passed on to us from generations before us. By training others effectively we have given others a skill and instill confidence in them; it also gives oneself a confidence that the learning's and skills we have developed or learned will go on as a legacy.

This also gives us the freedom to learn new things and to refresh ourselves by letting go. When others are trained, can do what you do, your time and skills are leveraged for your and societies benefit. The experiences that you had are replicated (with perhaps some innovations from your trainees) and you can now create new skills and applications supporting your creativity and innovative nature. All of what we know and impart to others helps future generations.

Language and Communication Skills

Communication skills are an essential part of our life, livelihood, and success in business relationships. Languages are the gateway to knowing others and building relationships. We start out with a "native language." Some never progress beyond that but others learn at least one or more others, giving them more joy and options. In fact, having several languages in ones brain is also intrinsically valuable for brain functioning.

I encourage people to learn a new language. It shakes up the neurons and invokes new connections and associations throughout the brain; it also improves our native speaking ability because of the differences between languages. What we take for granted is brought up to ponder.
When I have learned new languages and taught English to non-native speakers, I have to wonder what certain phrases mean when having to dissect and explain them to the students, like "That dog don't hunt." "Between hell and high water." "Oodles."

In learning another language, we can better detail in what we intend to say to the other person. This greater clarity and specificity helps the other person better know what's going on inside your head – improving the relationship you are trying to create.

That closeness creates the human bond. Sharing our "mind space" with others binds people emotionally. There's also a way to maximize brain health using its communicative skills to create emotional ties. This can be called a kind of cerebral-brainstem merger.

We all have five senses but certain ones can become dominant and others weaker. Knowing that visual, auditory, and kinesthetic "touch and emotions" are the three primary modes for most humans is a key to more effective communication. Brought to us by Bandler and Grinder, and refined by others, the art and science of NLP is based on this observation and it is well to be cognizant of that when communicating in spoken, written, or nonverbal language with others.

Knowing the sense or mode, someone is operating in is like speaking the other person's native tongue. For example, if they are speaking in colors and images, reply in colors and images. That is the "native tongue" of this moment.

Pictures, sounds, and emotions are how we predominantly experience internal and external life and how we store memories. Of course, taste and smell are mixed in there as at times for a delicious (or noxious) accent! Speaking, speaking and writing and all the modes require many parts of the brain to fire and "speak to" each other. This integration creates a natural power and maximization of brain health. In turn, that makes for a better life for so many reasons.

Being able to experience the world in all ways, visual, auditory, gustatory, olfactory, emotionally, and with touch adds the fabric and vitality for a rich life. Vitality in this life is prolonged by exercising all the capacities of crossed sensory neuronal activity that keeps the neurons alive and memory in cognitive capacity intact. This is why learning and knowing about NLP is so important to enhance our life's experiences.

Importance of Habits and Patterns

Habits and patterns, as we have seen, are part and parcel of effective living. Habits include routines of eating, drinking water, exercising daily, walking and sitting with great posture, handwriting skills, to name a mere few. The more we are consciously aware of the habits and patterns we have established (burned into our nervous system) , the better we are able to choose to use the habit or not.

At the same time, knowing other people's habits and patterns helps us improving our relating and communicating to them, if we take the time and effort to do so. If we know others behaviors we can adapt how we interact with them and make a more positive connection with them. We also can empathize and identify with their circumstances more effectively and compassionately. So when I pull together all of my "listening" skills, knowing a mode someone uses, habits and patterns that make that person's life unique and special to them, and then communicate that back to them in an authentic and spot on way, communication I intend for the other person actually reaches them in a deep and clear way with less confusion and misunderstanding.

I also like to use the skill sets wrapped up in the BANK card system to understand how to communicate better with others. To speak in their language. You can learn more about that system and how to apply it to your own life after playing the personality / values card game. http://www.playbankcode.com/drjaybankrapportcards

Locking in Positive experiences

Everyone loves to have great experiences. Ones that make them feel happy, understood, taken care of, heard, listened to, supported, the center of attention, of the universe. When we can communicate with someone in such a way as they like to be spoken to and heard, that is a peak experience that has lasting positive impact on that person.

Or, perhaps the positive experience is a personal accomplishment that that person achieved – a great recital they nailed, a personal best in sports when everything felt right, a long journey ends up in a magical outcome, completing a project that others like, made a music composition that is unique and a hit.

These positive experiences are filled with emotion and when remembered later bring back that same positive feeling. In and of themselves they are strong memories, but when we take time to savor them, and even accentuate every aspect of the "win," they can become cornerstones of "power" that we can draw upon later when we need the energetic or emotional boost. When I am feeling defeated, I can draw on them. When I am feeling tired on a long car drive, I can draw on them and pull up a new alert and awaken state.

These good and bad emotional experiences can be boosting or depressing. If we are trying to learn something new, being in a good mood actually makes our learning easier. We learn better when we are feeling positive about ourselves. So knowing this, how can we improve our ability to help others around us to learn more effectively?

I took a course on accelerated learning and Blair Singer was one of the teachers. A method that he had taught in which I have passed on is the "yes" gesture. When I want to "up my game" or get out of an emotional funk that is not serving me, I draw on my many great experiences and wins by pumping my arm, using the fist pulling-down gesture, and say "Yes! Yes! Yes!" It works every time. I also do it with the opposite arm to get a stronger effect and to balance my brain integration.

How Others Know <u>Us</u>

Others know us by shared experiences. We are here at their birth. We assist and watch them as they learn to walk, talk, ride a bike, drive. When they have their first cold, first crush on someone, first "best friends" fight. A spat with a parent. An exhilarating ride at Disneyland or their first swim on their own without touching the wall or the bottom of the lake or pool. We feel a deep bond with others by sharing these events at the same time and place.

But, what about when we aren't there? We can't be there or hadn't even known the person before recently or just now. How can we establish, that deep, heart to heart, "I love that!" "I felt that!" "So sorry to hear that" – kind of closeness with another soul? Of course, by sharing it through speaking, talking together or just being a great listener. Hearing the nuances, seeing the shades, the place-time emotions, feeling their journey – the struggles, the losses, the triumphs, the regrets, and the joys. In the midst of that, we also have the experiences we share, similar times and our adventures, we can walk verbally together also through our life experiences so that they are with us there on the journey of our life experiences. We become bonded, linked, and closer by sharing our human experiences.

Whether together or in our own imaginations. The power of brain waves in sync. Bonding hearts and minds. Sharing intimacies. Life, real "and natural virtual." The mind linking with other humans that scientists say begins as early as 9 months of age in our personal development.

CHAPTER 2: HOW DOES YOUR NERVOUS SYSTEM WORK?

Introduction on Levels and Viewpoints of Existence and Function

How does something work? Answering that depends upon the perspective and viewpoint you are looking, listening, and feeling from.

In many decades long study of the human body, mind, spirit and emotions, as well as based on my academic and day-to-day experiences of life, I like most other humans have learned from others who have specialty training and focus. With a strong background in the medical sciences, I have studied biology, physics, chemistry, biochemistry, psychology, sociology, metaphysics, electromagnetic principles, and other disciplines and perspectives. I have gotten to learn the different levels and ways that we human "beings" operate. The important word here is "beings."

My discussion in this book of the development of the brain and body and how to enhance them will use many of these approaches and I will not necessarily distinguish which of them I am using at any one time. So, for example I will talk about cells and tissue structures that turn into the brain and nervous system. I will talk about the electrical activity of various parts of the brain (that comes from the coordinated activity of all the cells in that particular part of the brain), and I will also talk about some of the chemicals in the brain that are associated with production of energy, feelings of alertness and curiosity, and ones that reduce pain thresholds. We will also touch upon activities, various sensory stimulations from the "outside world," and about cultural constructs that influence and mold the individual.

Such are just some of the multilevel aspects of the brain. No one level or perspective tells the whole story and the whole story won't be written in this book due to the vastness of the whole subject. But I hope that at least some of the aspects will peak the interest and curiosity and satisfaction of your brain as it reads this.

Your Brain Studying Itself and a Brief Metaphysical Digression

Children are all naturally curious about the world. We were all once children and are still in fact children at some level because of layering of experiences and development of tissue structures over tissue structures. Our curiosity about the world continues our whole life unless damage or override of our innate curiosity tendencies or mechanisms occurs. Override here means things like physical traumas, emotional traumas, toxic assault, molestation, physical assault, PTSD, whiplash injuries, war injuries, living in environments of deprivation, et cetera.

Over time the debate has been "Where is the seat of the mind, of thought, of emotions?" Science and biopsychology will say that the brain is the focal point our body that organizes thought, emotion, and "knowing." It also wants to "Know" itself. What is the drive and motivation for this? We mention the curiosity all children have if they are healthy and nourished. But where does this curiosity and creativity spring from? Just the activity of the brain itself? Or something else?

Accepting that the brain is the "seat of knowing," I feel that its actual mechanism may be more closely linked to a concept of almost infinite black and white holes permeating that cranial space.
With that as the postulate (other brains are you following this?), one could then speculate that the energetic fields on the other side of the black and white hole "funnels" will drive the push to know how the brain works. Or, it could be curiosity, or even the drive to survive.

Knowing how the brain works may also lead to solutions to problems we can't solve yet and need to in order to survive as a species and as part of the whole environment.

But, let's set aside this black hole/white hole concept for the moment and go back to 4-dimensional reality discussion of the (4-dimensional) physical brain.

Maturation of the Brain Necessary for Self-Knowledge

On the other hand, the brain's capacity for self-knowledge is only possible with brain maturation. Maturation requires sufficient bodily movement/activity and sensory input to stimulate the creation of brain. The movement and sensory input is also required to integrate the different parts of the brain that are needed to work in conjunction to learn and figure out things -- ike how the brain works.

Maybe we have five senses because we have five fingers. We are able to live and even thrive at times with less than five (six). But what about having greater than five senses? What would the others be called and what were they pick up on in reality? Would they help with our survival or thriving?

Focusing on Time-Space Dimensions of Reality for Now

Regardless, we do know that our primary senses have corresponding brain structures: smell and taste with the olfactory nerve, sight and vision with the optic and oculomotor nerves, hearing with the auditory nerve, touch with many nerves in the brain stem and the peripheral nervous system. And yet the order of the nerves, from top to bottom, is not directly related to prioritization of senses needed for survival today in modern urban life. We're talking here about the 12 cranial nerves.

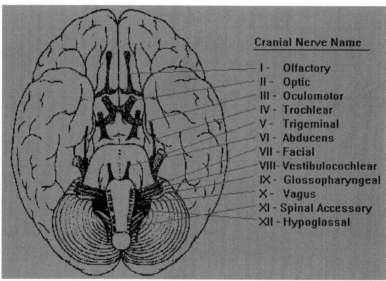

Source: Faculty.washington.edu

The cranial nerves are listed below and the picture of where they connect into the brain is shown on the previous page.

From cranial nerve 1 to 12, the nerves are in this order: I. olfactory, II. optic, III. oculomotor, IV. trochlear, V. trigeminal, VI. abducens, VII. facial, VIII. Vestibulocochlear, IX. glossopharyngeal, X. vagus, XI. spinal accessory, and XII. Hypoglossal. All of these cranial nerves (nerves that exit the central nervous system inside the skull or cranium) enter and exit the brain stem.

Movement needed for Brain Development

Moving causes stimulation of brain development. Feeling, seeing and hearing our bodily movements stimulates brain development. Crawling, rolling over, sitting, standing, walking, throwing, catching, and running are all necessary to develop the mature nervous system.

Sensory Input

Sensory input is fundamental to being alive. Seeing, hearing, smelling, tasting, and touching form the five basic senses, with intuition often referred to as our sixth sense. (Dr. Robert Melillo calls the 6th sense is the ability to perceive of and adjust to gravity, which is totally different thing from intuition). Some of us operate extraordinarily with loss of 1, 2, or even three senses. I don't know if many people have lost 4 or five of their senses without being dead or in a deep coma. The dead are not alive and those in a coma can't be considered to "have a life" as we know it. They are alive but they don't have much of a life. Based on this line of logic we can definitely say that sensory input is fundamental to being alive.

The Elephant Story

There is a story about four blind men feeling and sensing an elephant. Each has a different perception of what the elephant is. Put them all together and there is a "complete picture," or is there? Sight, sound, taste, smell, touch. And some would argue intuition being the sixth sense.

Why only Five Senses?

But why did we develop these five sensory mechanisms and not others? Humans living on and being a product of being on planet Earth, have had to survive and thrive. Revolving around the axis and around the sun, we developed a capacity to sense light. The sun produces heat also, so we developed touch sensation.

Various natural sounds - of other animals, earthquakes, the undercover landslide, rain, bubbling springs and rivers, waves, wind through the trees - being able to hear these before seeing them has its advantages. Not to mention the sound of engines, rockets, gunfire, voices, drums, etc.

Rotting food, dangerous material and synthetic chemicals - all of these emit smells that our nose alerts us to. Soured milk, rancid oils, extremely bitter seeds, extreme acids and bases, these all are taste warnings to beware of and avoid to prevent illness or even death. Because we eat and consume to survive and prevent illness or even death.

Because we eat and consume to survive, the oral portal guard of taste (with smell, sight, and sound) are again the guardians of bodily harmony. Not to mention all of the sights, sounds, smells, tastes, and touch - feelings that we really enjoy -- bring pleasure and bring great fulfillment with -- let's not forget the positives!

So that tells us a little about why the five senses are primary for physiological human development. Survival and superthrival.
But why not more senses? What senses might we have or need that are not an obvious component of our nervous system? Well, I mentioned intuition. The apparent ability to sense (or just know) that something will happen in the future. The possibility to plan or anticipate an event and take action can be very helpful to thrive or survive – or to help others do so.

Indeed, many stories of religion and culture are based on such sensory powers. Many posit a direct connection with a god, gods, or higher power not of the earth. Who hasn't had an experience of intuition? I know no one I've spoken to around the world who hasn't had an extra sensory perception. But besides intuition, what other senses should, or might we humans have?

Prioritization of the Senses

But of the five majors senses, some of us use some more than others. It seems that some people tend to be highly motivated by visual experience, like artists, architects, beauty contest and clothing fashion professionals. Others may be drawn to and rely more on hearing and sound experience. Such as musicians, speakers, orators, actors, singers.

And there are also the smellers - the olfactory and tasters. The perfume developers, the chefs, the wine tasters and smellers.

There are also the touchers -- those who hug, or want to hug, everyone they meet, the acupuncturists, surgeons, massage therapists, dancers, wrestlers, boxers, soccer players, hockey players, swimmers - most sports figures. The special expertise built on a particular sensory dominance is indisputable. And yet, a mixture of all the senses to greater or lesser proportions is vital for a high performance life.

By <u>consciously</u> understanding the divisions of sensory experience and how each of us integrates those in each task we perform, it is possible to improve how we operate, enhancing our brain health for a better life.

Technologies that help us understand these tendencies to use particular senses include neurolinguistic programming (NLP). The politician's best speech, the salesperson's script, the website copywriters story, all are more impactful and influential when these senses are all touched upon in what is seen, heard, and felt by the target audience. Developing these senses of our brain is a key component of proper neurological development and methods used to enhance and optimize brain health as well as approaches to teaching others in schools and on the job.

Brain FAQS and Statistics

Your human nervous system is looked at broadly as having 3 divisions, the central nervous system, the autonomic nervous system, and the peripheral nervous system.

The central nervous system (CNS) is composed of your brain, brain stem, cranial nerves, and spinal cord. The autonomic nervous system regulates organ function based on two "competing" or "balancing" sides – the sympathetic and the parasympathetic. And the peripheral nerves are the nerves extending out from the spinal cord, out from and back to the spinal canal (encircled in bone) to the farther reaches of the body, like the arms and legs, fingers and toes.

The *long term development* of our human nervous system has certain milestones according to archeologists:

7,000,000 (7 million) years ago our spinal cord moved forward in bony structures (creating greater protection)

2,000,000 (2 million) years ago we started using tools and created homes

1,000,000 (1 million) years ago we started having a large brain

100,000 (1 hundred thousand) years ago we gained the ability to use symbols to relay information. This laid down the foundation for the development of language and writing, a skill we are using at this moment.

Growing Size of the Human Brain Over Geological Time

The brain size of humans has gotten proportionally larger, giving us greater and greater capacity to put "one and one" together. Between 2 million and 1 million years ago our brain size doubled. Between 1 million years ago and 200,000 years ago our brain size doubled again. Thus, compared to 2 million years ago, our brain is now 4x larger.

It is approximated that there are 90-100 billion nerve cells in the brain. The connections between the brain cells, the neurons, are called synapses. There may be as many as 500-1,000 trillion synapses that are the connections between the different nerve cells that are a physical structure associated with the different ways that our nervous system connects memories, experiences, sensory input, and activities into a fully functioning movement and thought control center.

"Western Scribjay" or Thinking about our own Thinking

The ability to identify the state of your knowledge – thinking about thinking – is known as metacognition. This is exactly what we are doing together at this moment. We are thinking about how thinking occurs. Physically, our brain is the master organ of this process and nerve cells, neurons, are the components that biologically create the network of associations that process input and create memories of complex patterns of sensory experiences.

Living in trees

As a child did you climb trees? Almost every child I know of climbs trees, and many movies incorporate this tree climbing as a part of it (think Twilight with Bella and Edwards' climb up the tall tree). It can be a challenge to climb a tree, and unless one is afraid of climbing, it is really quite fun. Tree houses are also a part of many children's experience (it was in mine) and they are found in many movies as well, like High School Musical. What is this fascination with climbing and being up in trees? Could it be an echo of the point in time when our genetic ancestry lived in trees?

The Development of the Larger Human Brain

The emerging larger brain became more hungry for energy in order for it to work. This is thought to be based on the ability to rely more on animal fats and animal proteins.

Studies comparing children and various primates has shown that human (children – and thus adults as well) have an innate "shared intentionality" that is shown in a sampling of vegetarian fare (food). This shared intentionality is one person having the ability to know what another person knows when looking at a small object while playing a game. This linking of minds and understanding is something that seems to be unique to humans.

The untutored child around the age of 2, the "toddler" has been chosen to study our innate cognitive skills." It is considered to be "innate" at this time because no formal education has occurred up to that point in most situations. This is before the child masters language or is exposed to formal schooling. We already talked about this in Chapter 1.

Electrical Properties of the Brain

Research in the middle of the 1900's first measured the electrical properties of the human brain. Studies conducted with electrodes attached to the scalp measured the electrical waves emanating from the brain during different brain activities. Subjects who were meditating produced electrical waves of a predominantly 8-12 hertz frequency. Hertz is a measure of the number of waves per second seen on an oscilloscope. While there were other frequencies showing up, this frequency range was by far the most prominent. These were called "alpha" waves. I assume that they were called "alpha" waves because they were the first brain waves discovered and measured. Later on, other wave patterns and ranges were measured and discovered, and then these were also labeled with Greek letters. We discussed this in more detail previously in this chapter. Refer back to the chart on frequencies, although it does not show the higher frequencies up to 100 Hz.

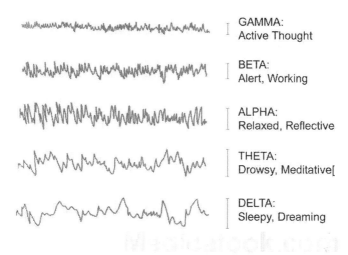

GAMMA:
Active Thought

BETA:
Alert, Working

ALPHA:
Relaxed, Reflective

THETA:
Drowsy, Meditative[

DELTA:
Sleepy, Dreaming

Our brain and other parts of the body produce electrical energy that can be measured. The heart's electrical rhythms are measured with an EKG, electrocardiogram. And our muscles move due to changes in electrical charge movements causing a ratcheting effect.

A question many patients wonder is "When one part of the brain is more active and we can measure high electrical activity corresponding to that area or functional aspect of the brain, are the other parts still working?" All parts of our brain are working all the time but to different degrees. When we are sleeping there is a predominance of slower wave patterns, the delta and theta. When we are coming out of sleep, day-dreaming, meditating or praying, we have the alpha wave predominance pattern. When we are "eyes wide open" awake, we have a predominance of beta wave activity. Beta wave is in the 14-24 hertz range, twice as fast as the alpha wave. But, there are still other wave patterns occurring at the same time as the dominant wave pattern – they are just at a lesser level.

The Brain Likened to a Radio

I liken this to a radio and radio waves. With a radio we have a choice to tune in to a particular channel – whether FM or AM band. Let's say it is the FM band, the "frequency modulation" band. At one end of the band are the slower frequencies, the lower numbers on the dial. At the other end of the dial are the faster frequencies, the higher numbers. We can't listen to all of the stations across the band at the same time with one radio. We have to select. However, it doesn't mean that the others aren't there to listen to potentially – we just have to select which frequency / station we want to listen to at the moment. Our brain and its operation are somewhat similar. Your brain has a little more ability to mix the stations compared to a radio receiver, but one station comes in the loudest. And the more we focus in on that station the better it performs.

This channel selection process in our brains is what I call "attention and awareness." Our individual human ability to put our attention and awareness at a particular level of operation and then carry out the functions that are inherent and associated with that particular "station's programming." Like meditation, sleep, dreaming, being wide awake and talking or reading (like you are doing at this moment.) Of course, that is not to say that the other "stations" or levels of consciousness are not operating simultaneously and in parallel, because they are. There just isn't as much juice in them. So, for example, the part of the nervous system that keeps the heart pumping and lungs inhaling and exhaling continues operating all the time even if we are not thinking consciously about it. Those are like the power box, CPU and operating system of a computer, always running in the background (unless the plug gets pulled. The "juice " is always there at a survival level, and one can actually learn to consciously control heart rate with practice, but the base line of that "radio station" is not so strong as to be a dominant.

So that is my radio tuner analogy to better explain the idea of the multi-level electrical frequency activities of the brain and how we can course up and down the dial either consciously or unconsciously, with our awareness-attention field focus being the determining factor of the station or dominant frequency our brain is expressing at any moment in time.

Amplifying Your Brain's Alpha Wave State

Various systems of meditation, guided imagery, hypnotherapy and other similar practices will product an alpha wave dominant brain emanation. This is why, for example, in the Silva method they deliberately and directly state and refer to the "alpha" state while leading, practicing and engaged in the practices.

Enhancing brain activity and functioning is partially accomplished by balancing and uptuning the two sides of the brain. There are various technologies invented to do this, and they consist typically of audio tracks that "sync" (Synchronize) the two sides of the brain using specific sounds, rhythmic patterns of a particular frequency. Given that each of our nervous systems and bodies developed the first 9 or so months in an internal environment with the constant rhythmic sound of a heart beating in particular ranges of frequencies (50 to 160, with a typical base line somewhere around 72 beats per minute), a rhythmic sound in even sub-audible levels will impact the activity of the brain. Then, using headphones or ear buds, with a variation in the sounds coming in from each side, helps to stimulate the opposite acoustic nerves connected to the ears and auditory sensing and analyzing areas of the two sides of the brain.

There are systems to use visual stimulation in particular patterns to help to retune the brain as well. Linking up visual patterns with the rhythm of an individual's heart rate has shown in research studies to also have positive effects on the executive functions of the brain, reduce stress responses, and enhance memory and decision making. Here again, we are using a primary sensory input, here being visual, in a rhythmic frequency, to effect the brain and enhance its function. Sounds are also used in association with the visual stimulation to enhance the brain tuning effects. Further information on these systems mentioned above are available online at www.superbrain-thebook.com. We will touch on these again in Chapter 8 as well.

Starting from One and Going to Billions

"In the beginning there was one. Then there came the great separation, the Yin and the Yang."

"The Tao that can be spoken of is not the true Tao."   Tao Te Ching

The start of the building of our human bodies is the moment of conception – namely, when a sperm and egg meet and the sperm is invited into the egg. This can now occur in the test tube, and as of now we don't know of any other method being used to start the development of a human body (and being.) In other words, cloning of humans is not happening at least in the eyes of the common person.

This merging of a sperm and an egg, and the genetic mingling of two halves of a whole chromosomal structure in and of itself does not define a human being that is viable. Much more has to happen before that can be said. And even after birth and maturation there are factors that could be lacking that would enable an individual human being to exist "on their own, independently." It is all relative, because all of us need others around us to survive and thrive no matter what our abilities.

At any rate, how do we get from two cells into one cell and then to the person reading this book right now?

So, like the progression of Chinese medicine systems, from the Tao Te Ching to the Hexagrams, from one cell, to two (Yin and Yang), to four, to eight (the Trigrams), to 16, to 32, to 64 (the Hexagrams of the I Ching), to 128, to 256 (does this not bring to mind the development of computer RAM, etc?), 512, 1024, 2048, etc. Until the body is ready to be born, at anywhere from 1 million to 1 billion cells (estimated by various sources).

So during this process, like all parts of the body, the nervous system progressed from more primitive stages to more mature.

The development of the embryo into a human being with self-sustaining functioning is called embryological development. There are connections established between cells during the embryological stage that persist into a mature human being in spite of the fact that the cells are no longer next to each other and are not even in the same tissue structure. There are various pain syndromes that we have found that are not definable from strictly a nerve connection relationship. This is an example of "embryological connection."

Now, previously we talked about the increasing numbers of cells created by cell division and yet still connected together. At first cells have potential to become almost any other kind of cell. This is a stem cell or pluripotent cell. Lots of potential to become any kind of cell in the body. Something like the potential that each baby has to learn to take on almost any kind of job or to learn to speak any language they are exposed to. Later on in various stages of embryological development the cells become more and more specialized by a progression of steps.

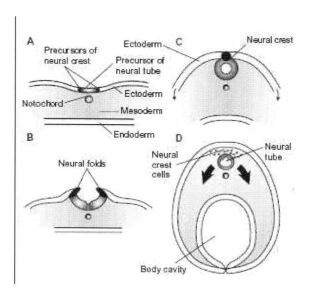

http://missinglink.ucsf.edu/lm/IDS_101_embryology_basics/images/neural_tube_cross_section.gif

Neurological development goes through stages, and these stages are associated with the formation of cells in certain structures. The names of these include the ectoderm, notochord, neural tube, brain stem, diencephalon, neocortex, etc. Illustrations of some of those early stages are shown on the previous page. As more and more cells are produced to create new and more specialized nervous system structures, our abilities as developing human beings expand – after birth our nervous system continues to get more cells with more specific functions as well as connections and integrations of the different functions.

Later stages of change, that represent the archetypal shape of the brain reading this right now, are shown next. Parts of the brain are labelled.

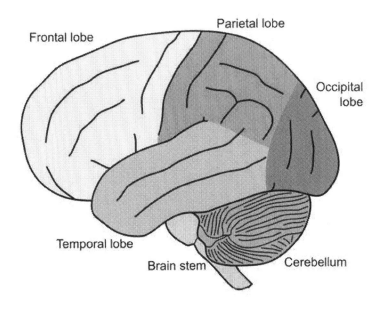

Source:mycafelyrics.com

The different lobes are parts of the cerebrum, also called the "neocortex." Also visible is the cerebellum, and area that coordinates movement, thoughts, and functions; note that the brain stem is partially shown and is not visible here, but largely resides inside the neocortex.

Just as societies and countries that have designed and created pyramids and space ships to go to the moon had to have sufficient numbers of people doing certain functions with certain knowledge, the nervous system has to have sufficient numbers of cells of various types that have undergone particular experiences to be able to carry out their functions. People making the pyramids had to have food and water and movement and coordination of effort to make the pyramids. Our nervous system likewise has to have the nutrients, oxygen, water, stimulation, and coordination to do things like singing, dancing, riding a bicycle, reading, writing, and remembering.

I think that it bears repeating: our nervous system is divided into three main divisions, the central nervous system, the peripheral nervous system, and the autonomic nervous system. The central nervous system being the brain and spinal cord (enveloped by 3 membranes called the meninges). The peripheral nervous system is all of the nerve tissue that extends out from the spinal cord. These transmit sensory messages from the periphery (distant from the center) to the central nervous system and transmit muscle activity messages (motor nerves) from the spinal cord or brain to cause muscles to lengthen or contract. The autonomic nervous system regulates the functioning of organs and is associated with the stress / relaxation responses of the body.

So in order to enhance brain health for a better life ALL of these 3 divisions of the nervous system have to be taken into account in addition to all other parts of the body which are connected up to and communicating with the brain and central nervous system.

Humans as a Product and Reflection of Nature

Let's go back a little in our nervous system development discussion. We humans are a reflection of and outgrowth of nature. We have observed that the development of the central nervous system looks somewhat like the development of a tree. The primary parts of the central nervous system are the brain stem (trunk) diencephalon (main branches), spinal cord (tap root), and the neocortex (cerebellum, cerebrum, and everything between these and the brain stem) being the smaller branches and leaves. Watching the development of a head of cauliflower is also a beautiful analogy.

The bottom line is that the higher levels of human functioning, like that of complex language, ability to build and create things, self-reflection (like what we are doing right now), memory and manipulating ideas "in our head" all emerge from the brain stem and survival functions.

The brain stem is the survival brain. The place that basic heart and lung function is regulated initially. The place that primitive reflexes of suckling and grasping occur. They are natural reflexes that cause a baby to grasp onto your finger and start sucking it when it is young. A survival instinct. As stated before, all of our senses from the outside world, the world that is outside of our individual skins, are filtered and passed through the brain stem. These nerve impulses and messages pass through the brain stem on their way to the higher branches of the brain "tree" or are dealt with in the brain stem itself from a "survivalist" perspective. The nerves of vision, hearing, smell, taste, all pass through the brain stem associated areas before going to the higher areas that analyze and classify and compare based on experience and memories. Thus, when enhancing brain health taking the brain stem and survival brain into account can make the difference between high level functioning and less high level functioning.

The fact that all of the higher intellectual, emotional, cognitive, language, and spiritual functions as symbolized by the neocortex exfold from the brain stem embryologically, the brain stem has a dominating influence over our basic beingness. The start of our maturing stage of physical/natal development is the brain stem.

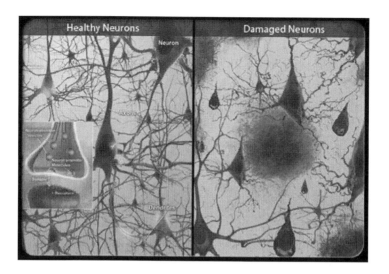

It is said that there are 500 TRILLION synaptic connections in the brain. (Richard Restak, Professor of Neurology, George Washing University School of Medicine and Health Sciences). Robert Melillo DC says it is 1,000 trillion. Whichever number it is, synaptic connections are the places where the arms (axons) of the nerve cells come close together and communicate across a gap.

But it takes quite a while for that to happen. The development of your brain starts with two cells for the entire body. Because your brain doesn't develop in isolation, it is an essential outgrowth with all the other organs, systems, and structures of your body.

So two cells (usually) intersect; the sperm enters the ovum. These two become one and then divide into two cells that are a special combination of the initial two. Then each of the following cells divides in two. 4, 8, 16, 32, 64, 128, much like the progression of computer chips and storage. There are significant milestones along the way, at week 2, at 1 month, etc.

I already mentioned the mesoderm, endoderm, and ectoderm, the primordial tissue structures that transform into more differentiated organ structures and systems that are the basis for some of the disease associations seen in children and adults.

And then those changing into neural tube, and exvolution of the "over brain," the cerebrum, from the survival-brain brain stem. Like a tree growing branches and leaves and a tap root (the spinal cord).

All the while this is going on in the context and environment (within the mother's womb) of sounds of pulsing blood, beating heart, intestinal sounds, music, voices, silence.

Then at sometime around 6 weeks or later of pregnancy there is a beating heart in the developing fetus as well, so that rhythmic sound and feeling is locked into the developing nervous system and vibrational memory. Please note here that this feeling is a vibrational sensation as hearing is a vibrational sensation. (And vision is vibrational waves of light, but in utero there is not light hitting the developing eye as we know it outside the mother's womb).

There is tactile stimulation of the outside of the developing body, skin layers, as the skin develops, expands, and presses against the placenta and the internal textures of the mother.

All parts of the brain and nervous system, all of the nervous tissue cells evolving from the original cells which were exposed to all the sounds, impressions, emotions, and motions/movements that the mother was also exposed to during that 9 month period. All of these have an impact on the developing nervous system and brain. Thus it is also said that the preconception states of the mother and father have a determining influence on the personality tendency of the child.

The Chemical Environment Influence on the Brain

The chemical environment the child develops in literally in the uterus has major influences on the brain health and the life of the child thereafter for better or for worse. Well known are the devastating effects on decreased learning abilities and disruptive behavior exhibited by babies developing in a mother who is using crack cocaine. In many school districts where the crack epidemic was severe, like parts of the San Francisco area where I practice, teacher patients of mine told me of the "wave of crack babies" that flowed through the school system. Teachers passed students on from grade to grade who were not up to grade standard simply because their brains and nervous systems were so negatively affected by crack cocaine during embryological development that there was only a limited ability of teachers to teach them. A number of years later there was a different wave of drug altered children that passed through. Similar difficulties in learning were observed in concerned teachers and parents.

We also know of the negative effects of alcohol on the fetus that alcoholic pregnant mothers cause to their babies, with alcohol addicted babies the result.

And we also know that blood lead tests are done on almost all children in certain public health programs because early detection and intervention in those children can help them overcome the long-term damage that will surely result to the brain when lead is consumed. Lead based paints and lead in gasoline has been banned due to this exact mechanism.

Other chemicals found in the umbilical blood of almost all children tested by the Environmental working group, chemicals that can have powerful neurological and other toxic effects on the body, are in every child born now. So this has to be taken into account when we are trying to maximize brain health for a better life.

After Birth

At the time of birth, the heart is already beating. The lungs then have to kick in and work to start providing the oxygen in the blood that the baby needs to have for the brain and other parts of the body to function and produce energy. So this brand new starting of the function of the lungs requires a rapid heart rate and breathing rate. Over time the heart and breathing rate of the person slows down due to various mechanisms.

With the start and continuation of neural development there are basic reflexes that control breathing and heart rate. The medulla, in the brain stem, controls and propagates these vital reflexes. Breathing and heart rate are rapid at early ages of development. Most functions of the infant are still run from the brain stem areas as the cerebrum is getting larger and can start to assume a greater role. As these higher brain function develop, they inhibit and can override the medullary reflexes. Reflexes are just arcs of nerve reaction without inhibition. For example, hit below your knee cap with a small rubber hammer or the side of your hand and the knee should start to straighten (kick out) without hesitation of or prompting by thought. This is a type of reflex.

This inhibition (of the brain stem reflexes running the fast heart rate) allows and causes slower heart rate and breathing rate. Blood pressure is also the same. It is a vital sign and function. If heart rate and breathing rate slow down at rest, it means that the higher brain is not functioning properly. Oppositely, blood pressure should also gradually rise to a healthy level when the higher cortical function is working. If not, it tells us that the primitive functioning is still dominant. And a domination of brain activity by the primitive function is not maximizing brain health – being dominated by the primitive and survival (sub conscious) brain leads to low social and professional functioning.

Of course, we want all parts of the brain to work in a coordinated fashion, just like all of the radio stations a radio could pick up are all potentially there at the same time all the time. We just have particular radio stations, frequencies, that we want to or need to listen to at a particular time. That is like the brain, with a dominance of activity in the 14-25 Hz range when we are thinking, talking, and listening, or moving. All at the same time or not.

The lower frequency activities are there creating influence and necessary for the processing of sound, sight, taste, smell, and touch, but they are not dominant.

On the other hand, that dominance of the lower frequency activities are exactly what is necessarily going on in the infant.

Uneven Development of the Two Hemispheres of the Cerebrum

The neocortex (cerebrum) has various lobes as shown on a previous picture. It also has two halves, hemispheres on the left and the right sides inside the skull. Each side has particular functions that it specializes in and has to coordinate with the other side for us to function optimally. (Are you catching this? Yes, you, the brain that is reading this!) A balanced stimulation of all the functions managed by both sides is necessary for you to operate in full gear. And to shift gears easily. A predominance of development of one hemisphere to the detriment of the other will result in uneven abilities to do various tasks.

For example, blood pressure between the two sides of the body should be about 10 points at most different. If there is one side that is more than 10 points higher it tells us that that side of the brain is weaker. Why is this? The hemisphere's job is to inhibit the brain stem reflex controlling heart rate and blood pressure. If it is not developed enough, it can't control the brain stem reflex and thus it is not inhibiting the blood pressure.

The two hemispheres do not development evenly during a normal progression of the nervous system. Major developmental milestones include rolling over, sitting up, standing, walking and saying those first few words. There are also specific milestones noted at the end of month one, end of the third month, end of 7th month, by first birthday, and by end of second birthday for infants and toddlers. It is at this time that the predominant development of the right hemisphere starts to take less emphasis and the left hemisphere starts to kick in more. Gross motor (big muscles, big actions) activity is controlled by the right hemisphere, and rolling over etc. is a big motion activity (compared to hand writing, for example).

Primitive reflexes should be gone by age 1.

There is also a right side or left side of body dominance that a person develops that is normal. If there is a crossed pattern this may indicate lack of coordination of the nervous system. This dominance is related to the hand, foot, eyes, and ears.

A head tilt shows a weakness and lack of coordination of the brain hemispheres. The side of the tilt is usually the weaker hemisphere.

Academic milestones are also observable and key markers at various times of childhood: age 6 months, 8 months, ten months, one year, 18 months, age two, age 2, three, four, and five. After that, there are academic standards measured in formal schooling settings or home schooling. These ranges include preschool, kindergarten through grade 4, grades 5 – 8, and grades 9 – 12. Remembering again, a full complement of brain waves from 1 Hz

(Hertz) to 24 Hertz should kick in by age 24, so up to grade 12 is just up to 18 Hertz.

For example, word reading is a left brain skill. Reading comprehension is a mixture of left and right brain skills, but more so right than left. Sounding out words, especially fake words, is a left brain skill because it is auditorially based. Numerical operations is more a left-brain skill. On the other hand, a typical "Math wizard" is a right brain dominance and decreased left brain ability. Math reasoning involves both sides of the brain. Spelling is more left brain oriented, written expression is a mix, listening is a mix but generally more right, and oral expression is a mixture of both, but right brain delay has a bigger impact.

Right brain deficiency always shows up as behavioral issues first. A left brain deficiency usually shows up as an academic problem.

These are just some of the observations and facts to take under consideration when we want to maximize brain health for a better life.

Hopefully your brain is enjoying this as much as my brain does. Learning about itself and how it works!

A summary of some of the major differences in the right and left hemispheres is shown in this table.

Right and left brain characteristics and contrasts

<u>Right Hemisphere</u>	<u>Left Hemisphere</u>
Big Picture	small picture
nonverbal communication	verbal communication
big muscle control	small muscle control
EQ	IQ
comprehension	word reading
math reasoning	math calculations
interpreting information	processing information
unconscious actions	conscious actions
negative emotions	positive emotions (responds to)
low frequency sound	high-frequency sound
high frequency light	low frequency light
interpreting auditory input	receiving auditory input
understanding abstract concepts	Linear and logical thinking
cautious and safe actions	curious and impulsive actions
likes newness and novelty	likes routine, sameness
suppresses immunity	activates Immunity
spacial awareness	
senses of taste and smell	
social skills	
Digestion	
computer games loved	
Depression	
more quiet	
Abstract art	
Autoimmune disorders	

(From "Disconnected Kids," by Robert Melillo, DC)

A Review: Structures of Your Brain

Once again, I am going to be redundant for learning purposes. Please don't think that I am disrespecting your brain. My brain simply hopes that your brain will appreciate the review and recognition of how awesome it is! We are all resonating together as one system….

Some basic structures of the brain include the reptilian brain, the limbic brain and the neocortex. The latter two emerge from the reptilian brain in the course of neurological development of your brain tissue structures.

The reptilian brain is the brain stem and it is called this because it looks like the brain of a reptile and because it functions in the realm of survival, fight or flight responses, hunger or fear, attack or run. The limbic brain is on top of the reptilian brain and is also called the mammalian brain because this structure is only found in mammals on the Earth. It has more complex emotions, love, indignation, compassion, envy & hope – heart and gut feelings.

On top of both of them and developing out of the lower two is the neocortex, the new brain. It is the location of abstract though, words and symbols, logic and time. It is where many memories are stored to enable high level functioning like the production of sounds for language.

All of our sensory information comes in through the reptilian brain. We think first through the limbic brain and the decisions we make are based in small of large part on feelings. This is why sales people always say that emotion sells and logic justifies the emotional decision.

Our 5 senses transmit data directly to the reptilian brain which translates it into our primitive emotions. Then that data is passed on to the primitive emotions, then to the higher limbic and cortical brain to think and feel more complex things.

Because the sensory nerves are not distributed evenly in the body, some areas have more nerve endings than others. Like the face, fingers and feet. A diagram of that represents the relative numbers of nerves by increasing or decreasing the size of the part of the body shown. This is called a homunculus and the next picture shows that! I love this kind of chart.

How do you and your brain feel about what you just read and saw?

Communication involves all of this processing, with emotions, feelings, sight, sound, smells, tastes, and complex associations. The key to effective communication is to find the best story to use to convey your understanding of the world to the greatest number of people. I hope that you are understanding and smiling about what I am communicating to you, because, in the words of Thom Hartmann, "The meaning of communication is the response you get."

CHAPTER 3: Consequences of Brain Damage and Degeneration

There are numerous causes of damage and dysregulation of the brain. Damage and dysregulation of the brain can lead to various malfunctions, diseases and symptoms. These are the consequences. At one end of the consequences spectrum there are the annoyances and the problems that make life less easy and enjoyable – like (1) very mild memory difficulties, (2) slowing of the ability to do math calculations in your head (yes, you still do them in your head and not just on a calculator) or (3) difficulty figuring out how to drive to some place that you have been hundreds of times already.

At the other end of the consequence spectrum is severe stroke, severe dementia or Alzheimer's, paralysis of parts of the body, and even coma with no ability of the body to function without being hooked up to heart and breathing machines. Because the brain regulates and coordinates so many necessary functions in the body, damage or malfunction can lead to a host of problems.

Here we will discuss both the consequences and various causes of damage and dysregulation of your brain.

Some of the Consequences and Primary Signs of Brain Degeneration include:

Hypertension/High Blood Pressure

Poor Digestion

Allergies, food or otherwise*

Acid reflux*

Dry eyes and mouth*

Sexual Dysfunction

Erectile Dysfunction*

Hormone Imbalance

Increased Cholesterol*

Incontinence

Short-term Memory Issues

Memory Problems*

Reduced Ability to Learn

Mood Swings

Lowered Attention Span

Depression*

Fatigue

Lowered Creativity

Sleep problems*

Sleepiness when Reading

Reduced Comprehension

Inability to Handle Motion

(Like those crazy kids!)

Autoimmune disorders*

Difficulty Driving Due to Getting Lost

Memory loss that disturbs daily life, especially forgetting recently learned information.

Challenges in planning or solving problems that they are familiar with.

Difficulty finishing familiar tasks at home or at work. Or at leisure.

Confusion with time and place. Similar to what happens with concussion.

Trouble understanding visual images and spacial relationships.

New problems with words in speaking and writing.

Misplacing things and losing the ability to retrace steps.

Decreased or poor judgments.

Withdrawal from work or social activities.

Changes in mood and personality.

(Items marked with * can also be observed with unequal brain development as well as brain degeneration. The last 10 are also signs of progression of Alzheimer's)

Some of the Causes of Brain Damage, Brain Malfunction, and Brain Dysregulation

There is a very long list of the causes of the brain not working right. The list includes: imbalanced brain development, insufficient exercise, insufficient oxygen and nutrients getting to the brain, meningeal compression, immunological imbalances or inflammatory reactions, organic brain diseases, metabolic diseases such as thyroid disease and diabetes, heavy metal and chemical toxicity, stress reactivity and hypersensitivity, and physical and mental traumas. This list is by no means exhaustive, but it provides an idea about the kinds of conditions and causes that can many times be addressed and mitigated, if not reversed, to help a person return to a happier and satisfying life of independence.

Imbalanced Brain Development

Imbalanced brain development: You have already read about how our brains develop. Anywhere along the process of development there can be a trauma, overstimulation, under stimulation or other factor that can affect the brain and cause an imbalance in brain development. The imbalance or decreased neurological development can be minor, irrelevant, or a major problem for how you function in the now or future. It could cause a problem in processing or memory related to vision, hearing, taste, smell, touch or in functions such as speech, reading, writing, doing math, focusing, or putting things together with connections. So the brain can be slowed due to a variety of causes, and imbalanced brain development is one reason. Luckily, there are methods that are available to help overcome many of these brain imbalances if they are not too intracted.

Insufficient Exercise

We previously talked about the necessity of movement and exercise in the development and maintenance of your brain's (and your body's) health and function. In general, humans can increase the number of brain cells by running and aerobic exercise through a process called neurogenesis. When there is a brain imbalance, it is possible to use targeted physical exercises that stimulate the specific areas of the brain that are deficient. Often these exercises are done unilaterally, on one side only, to stimulate the side of the brain that is deficient. The exercises may engage specific senses alone, or they could be done using a combination of different senses combined, like vision and hearing and movement (kinesthetic). The exact exercises that need to be done are determined by a comprehensive evaluation of a person's brain function. On the other hand, when there is not a specific hemispheral weakness, a balanced exercise regimen is helpful to promote and maintain brain health.

Insufficient Oxygen and Nutrients Getting to the Brain

The methods also include nutrition and oxygen augmentation. We need to have sufficient energy and oxygen for our brain to work, right? The oxygen comes from the lungs and stores of iron in the form of hemoglobin in red blood cells. So if there is not enough oxygen the brain tissues, the nerves, can't repair themselves. Nutrients are also necessary to fix, repair, and optimize the functioning of the nerves. And to get the nutrients into the blood stream so they can travel through the arteries, between the meninges, and pass through the blood brain barrier into the brain tissues to be captured by the nerve cells. So the entire process of digestion is also very important for the health of the brain. Because if you can't get the right nutrients into the blood stream they can't be delivered to the brain. So dealing with any problems with the digestive system is a key method to help correct brain imbalances.

Meningeal compression

Meningeal compression can be a consequence of brain dysfunction and trauma. Meningeal compression can come from many physical causes: damage to the brain arising from car accidents, whiplashes, sports injuries from hits to head (baseballs, soccer balls, hockey pucks, baseball bats, elbows, knees), falls and post-surgical adhesions. Meningeal compression then can become the cause of numerous neurological problems. This is discussed in a separate chapter because of its significance and often being overlooked when evaluating the factors involved in a person's decreased functioning as presented in the clinic.

Organic Brain Diseases

Organic brain diseases include Down syndrome, fragile X syndrome, infectious and metabolic diseases or injuries, physical brain injury, strokes of brain tumors, psychiatric illness, personality disorders, and true brain disorders. There are various approaches that may be helpful for these diseases but other approaches, like the Brain Balance Program can't help these.

Immunological Imbalances or Inflammatory Reactions

The factors causing damage to your immunity include: stress, chemical toxicity, heavy metal toxicity, lack of exercise, fatigue, autoimmune disorders, use of steroids and NSAIDS that suppress the immune system, multiple vaccination shots (like those in Gulf War and Iraq war veterans), damage to the nervous system, obesity (causing slower healing from injuries), diabetes and metabolic syndrome, multiple medication use that weakens the immune system and the liver, poor diet, cancer chemotherapy, children having difficulty recovering from colds and ear infections, overuse of antibiotics, acquired immune deficiency syndrome (AIDS), radiation exposure on the job or environmentally, vitamin and mineral deficiencies, lack of sleep, parasitic infections of the blood and digestive system, imbalance in the acupuncture meridian system, weakness of the lungs and large intestine, deficient defensive energy, or "wei chi", residing in the skin and protecting the body from external pathogens, parasympathetic nervous system dominance, lupus, Hashimoto's thyroiditis, low thyroid, poor circulation, etc. The consequences of these can be any of the items listed in the list at the start of this chapter or many others. Thus, evaluation of these causes may be needed to get to the root of the brain problem and also should be addressed to maximize brain health and functioning.

Physical and Mental Traumas

Among the physical causes of brain damage and injuries, traumatic brain injury (TBI) and chronic traumatic encephalopathy (CTE) are two of the most commonly spoken about situations.

TBI can come from a variety of causes, such as sports injuries, moving vehicle accidents (cars, trucks, motorcycles), bicycle injuries, sports injuries when wearing or not wearing protective head gear, being hit in the head, falling and hitting the head, being assaulted , combat injuries and explosions, and even during the birthing process.

CTE can come from similar causes as TBI, but in this case it is the repetitive nature of the incidences that cause the injury is what is different. This is TBI in multiple situations that leads to a long-term, lasting result.

The consequences of head injuries, TBI, CTE and other more progressive brain damage from disease processes or medication effects is a huge list. Because the brain controls everything, having damage to the control center can cause a wide range of effects, from mild and almost not noticeable to severe results like PTSD, coma, symptoms of stroke, chronic pain, emotional distress like depression and even suicide.

Head injuries can lead to actual damage to the brain and its parts, like the meninges, but also other parts of the body, like hormones, muscles, tendons, ligaments and bones. They can severely impact a person's emotions, causing irritability, irrational behavior, and depression even leading to suicide. This is why carefully watching for unusual emotional changes is important in people who have had recent head injuries or multiple head injuries or concussions. This situation is seen often with professional football players, boxers, and hockey players who aggressively check each other.

Mental traumas are those related to events in one's life that impact the thinking and memories one stores. Psychological abuse, extreme situations like being a hostage, being held up at gunpoint, being in the middle of a war situation, a devastating earthquake or volcanic eruption, or in any number of other stressful extreme situations. The survival brain when in heightened alert scores these memories deeply into the psyche and then can be regurgitated up to overwhelm one in a moment totally unrelated to the trauma event. Nevertheless, that memory take over the internal reality of the brain and overshadow what is going on in the outside world. This process goes on to lesser degrees in many typical situations in life where our brain is comparing the new current situation with the others in the past that we have experienced in order to help determine how to respond to this new event. But when the old extremely traumatic memory is tapped into there can be a flood of emotions and old visual and other sensory impressions that overshadow any new input from the current moment. These types of extreme traumatic memories can end up paralyzing a person and preventing them from moving on with life and experiencing new situations with a freshness that makes them more successful. Some of the methods I cover in later chapters for optimizing brain health can be applied to break these old rigid memory patterns that lock a person in the past.

Metabolic Diseases

Metabolic disease such as thyroid disease and diabetes can be the consequence of brain damage but also can be the cause of brain dysregulation.

Either hyper or hypothyroid disease can cause our thinking and emotions to radically change and result in hyperactive behavior or sluggishness and depression. Memory can be decreased due to hypothyroidism as the energy levels needed to do mental work are reduced when the thyroid hormones are insufficient. Other consequences of thyroid disease can be lack of sleep and then the attendant inability of the brain to get to rest and reset itself and process the events of the day to create and sort out appropriate memories to store or discard.

Advanced diabetes has various negative impacts on the brain. High levels of sugar in the brain are pro-inflammatory and can cause "crusty brain syndrome" and a breakdown of brain cells due to inflammatory damage. Memory of people, places and things is damaged when blood sugar is out of control and too high; I have personally experienced relatives whose late stage diabetes resulted in them not knowing me or their children when I and they came to visit our diabetic relative in the nursing home. Diabetes is a cause of memory problems, not to speak of the toll it has on kidney function. When the kidneys are damaged and dialysis is required, the chemical changes in the body that results from kidneys not being able to filter nitrogen properly leads to changes in the thinking and behavior of the person with this problem.

Heavy metal and chemical toxicity

Many substances in the environment are neurotoxic. This means that they damage nerves and the brain which is composed of nerve cells. Well known neurotoxins include pesticides, volatile organic solvents, mercury, lead, aluminum, and cadmium. Clearing these chemicals and heavy metals out of our bodies is undeniably an important thing to do to reduce chances of memory loss, decreased brain ability and intelligence, tremors, Parkinson's, and other nasty degenerative conditions.

Toxins have always existed in our environment. Humans have learned which things make them sick and poison them, and which things make them healthy and strong. Sometimes it has been obvious; other times it has taken decades to really finally figure out that things we thought were health-producing are actually damaging to our bodies and brains.

Compared to 100 years ago, our environment is now filled with many more potential toxins. According to experts worldwide, there are more than 100,000 (one hundred thousand!) new chemicals in the environment that never existed before on this earth. That is because we humans created them to make things like cars, airplanes, computers, and cell phones. On the other hand, very few have actually been tested for their toxic or physical effects on the body, so their safety is unknown. These chemicals are man-made, artificial, not natural to the Earth. Think about it. Is your cell phone made of wood, plants, or parts of animals? While the chips are made of modified sand (silica), you just can't put together a cell phone by going out into the woods and collecting things from nature. So these 100,000 new chemicals are not natural and our bodies have never had to encounter them in the past. These chemicals are all new things for the immune system, cells, and tissues to figure out when the touch the body and if they get into the body. My chart below illustrates this extreme change over the past 100 years.

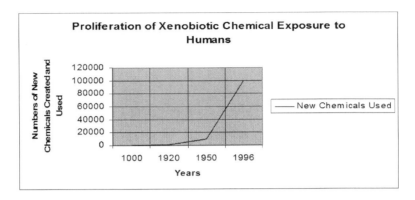

Chart: Proliferation of Xenobiotic Chemical Exposure to Humans

Other chemical toxins must be removed from our body to prevent nerve damage as well. Carbon tetrachloride, asbestos, pesticides, herbicides, and various plastics, to mention only a very few, are neurotoxic and cannot stay in our bodies without our expecting damage to be done. These chemicals can not only affect our thinking but how we feel and how able we are to move smoothly and painlessly. Nausea and vomiting are also possible primary effects of exposure to these chemicals that get into our body. A long list of chemicals that can be found in drinking water and their effects can be found at http://www.TheRedwoodClinic.com/toxins-in-water. A Multipure carbon block filter is tested to remove these substances to 99% by independent lab testing, so I recommend that all of my patients and people I care about to use this system for all their drinking and cooking water needs. http://www.multipureusa.com/redwoodclinic

There are certain primary organs and systems in our body that clear out toxins. Supporting our liver, gall bladder, bowels, kidney and spleen is a necessary and key memory care action to prevent chemical toxic buildup from killing us. Further information on this process is available in lectures

you may access through a special membership site
http://www.TheRedwoodClinic...com/clearing-toxins

Complete the <u>SURVEY below to see if you may have symptoms of toxicity</u>:

Enter the appropriate number - 0, 1, 2, or 3 - with 0 as least/never and 3 as most/always

___Acne and unhealthy skin

___Excessive hair loss

___Overall sense of bloating

___Bodily swelling for no reason

___Hormonal imbalances

___Weight gain

___Poor Bowel Function

___Excessively foul-smelling sweat

___ TOTAL

 If your total is 6 or more I suggest that you get evaluated more in depth.

SURVEY of Risk of Exposure

Enter the corresponding number

0=Never 1=Rarely 2=Monthly 3=Weekly 4=Daily

___How often are strong chemicals used in your home? (Disinfectants, bleaches, oven and drain cleaners, furniture polish, floor wax, window cleaners, etc.)

___How often are pesticides used in your home?

___How often do you have your home treated for insects?

___How often are you exposed to dust, overstuffed furniture, tobacco smoke, mothballs, incense, or varnish in your home or office?

___How often are you exposed to nail polish, perfume, hairspray, or other cosmetics?

___How often are you exposed to diesel fumes, exhaust fumes, or gasoline fumes?

___TOTAL

If your total is 8 or more I suggest that you get evaluated more in depth. See Chapter 12

SURVEY of Environment Factors

Enter the Corresponding number

0=NO 1=Mild Change 2=Moderate Change 3=Drastic Change

___Have you noticed any negative change in your health since you moved into your home or apartment?

___Have you noticed any change in your health since you started your new job?

Answer Yes or No (Yes = 4)

___Do you have a water purification system in your home?

___Do you have any indoor pets?

___Do you have an air purification system in your home?

___Are you a dentist, painter, farm worker, or construction worker?

___TOTAL

If your total is 8 or more I suggest that you get evaluated more in depth.

Stress Reactivity and Hypersensitivity

We all respond or react to life situations in various ways. We may be calm, or excited, or bored, or maybe even over-reactive. A new driver may get panicked when, as a passenger, the driver gets within a couple of car lengths from the car in front of their car. The experienced driver, on the other hand, has already taken her foot off the accelerator and has it poised over the brake, or on the brake, having responded to the new situation with seasoned and calm preparation. The passenger's heart rate accelerates, his shoulders and neck and back muscles get tense, he squirms and extends his arms out in front of him in preparation for the worst case possibility. The driver is nonplussed – breathing normally, speaking without a hint of anxiety, and laughing at the suggestion that there is any danger. The experienced driver responds to the situation; the inexperienced driver – passenger reacts. The reaction as described is a fight or flight stress response in which the adrenal glands are pumping out adrenaline and cortisol. When the stress response persists in a prolonged fashion, blood sugar levels rise, heart rate accelerates, memory for current events sharpens, and ultimately sleep is made more difficult. Without sleep long term memory conversion is inhibited and overall cognitive function is diminished. Sleep deprivation can lead to all kinds of emotional outbursts and foggy thinking.

Stress reactions are known to also diminish the ability of most people to take tests at their optimal level – memory and thinking is clearer if the stress reaction is modulated and not allowed to get to a point of panic and anxiety.

Cortisol's releasing of sugar loads into the blood stream is physiologically appropriate for a danger situation but when the sugar loads stay high there is an inflammatory result. Prolonged high sugar loads are known to damage brain cells, adding to the potential for a degeneration of the brain. Addressing stress reactions and training oneself to have stress responses instead is possible in many circumstances and will be discussed in greater detail in the chapter on enhancing brain function.

Difficulty Driving Due to Getting Lost

For many people, the ability to move around freely and get to places you want to when you want to leads to learning how to drive. Once a person has the skills of driving and can afford the costs of vehicle maintenance, insurance, etc., drivers are loathe to give up their power and independence. However, one of the consequences of Alzheimer's and dementia is the loss of the ability to remember how to get to even familiar places. This skill requires not only long term memory but tracking where you are at each step of the way. Alzheimer's can rob you of the coordination of those two skill sets. Losing one's license to drive and having one's car taken from them by loved ones is an emotionally difficult situation for the person with dementia as well as for the loved ones. There are standard scales of dementia that can be used to help determine when the driving should cease, for the safety of the driver and the safety of others on the road. Doctors sometimes use the Clinical Dementia Rating (CDR) scale to determine dementia severity.

Severe dementia has a CDR score of 3; moderate is 2; mild dementia is 1; and very mild is 0.5. Decisions about driving are clear-cut for people with CDR scores of 3 or 2: Professionals agree that anyone whose dementia is beyond the mild stage should not be allowed to drive. There is also agreement that individuals with very mild dementia (a CDR of 0.5) can continue behind the wheel. The gray area: mild-stage dementia (a CDR of 1). Studies show that as many as 76 percent of people with mild dementia could pass an on-road driving assessment. When the driver does go missing most are found in or near their parked car -- often a good distance from home. That could be in a different state or county.

If you think that your loved one might have Alzheimer's and could become lost, keep information and pictures of them and their vehicle available and know about the Alzheimer's Association's Safe Return Program, a nationwide alert service that assists law enforcement in finding missing individuals (http://www.alz.org/care/dementia-medic-alert-safe-return.asp).

CHAPTER 4: Symptoms of Meningeal Compression

We have previously mentioned the meninges, what they are and where they are located. These membranes are not considered to be pivotal by most physicians. In fact, the meninges are not on the radar screen as a problem for any condition unless the physician is a neurosurgeon or unless the person is suspected of having a severe headache due to meningitis. Nevertheless, the experiences I have had clinically, and those of hundreds of other skilled practitioners across the country, have led us to understand the importance of those 3 membranes in the health of brain and nervous system function.

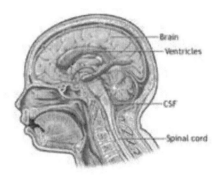

The meninges in a cross section of the head and skull

Ventricles are open spaces in the brain containing cerebrospinal fluid. The ventricles are lined with the meninges, the meninges being membranes that are like a plastic lining put in a large swimming pool, separating the concrete walls of the pool from the water. Cerebrospinal fluid is a liquid that circulates within the brain ("cerebro") and spinal cord ("spinal"). The circulation is contained within the meninges.

My Story: How I learned about Meningeal Compression

I am a widely trained student of life and how things work. My biography lists some of the medical practices that I have had the great privilege to have studied all around the world. Many of the natural medicine approaches I have learned hold great real promise and results for many people. But there is always something new to learn that may help even more people. That is how I came to learn about NRCT.

I was at a seminar where this fairly new method was being introduced. I sat watching videos of people who had some of the most difficult to treat conditions but made documented (right on the video) improvements over time when many other traditional approaches had either gotten just so far or the doctors had given up hope of any change. The case that got to me most was that of a teenage girl whose arm had to be weighted down to keep it from flapping. She had been to numerous neurologists who could only come up with the weighted bracelet solution. The moment she took off the bracelet her arm started flapping around. I believe that she was about the same age of my oldest daughter, and at that time she was in the 6-7th grade. I just imagined how going around with an arm that was totally uncontrolled would have stigmatized my daughter. Deep tears welled up inside of me in sadness for the girl with the flapping arm.

Then, with treatment using NRCT, this girl regained control of her flapping arm. It was a miracle as far as I was concerned. The girl's mother also told of a story of her "newly minted" daughter running again with free abandon – an action the mother at first was scared to allow her to do least she injure herself. Watching and hearing her story, liberation from the shackles and bondages of a lead wrist brace, moved me to tears of joy. So, in spite of the significant time and monetary commitment training involved, I pledged to myself and my patients to move forward and applied to study NRCT. I wanted to be the source of liberation for even more of the people I have the honor to work with over the years. The rest is history.

So, back to the discussion on meningeal compression. (You can also watch the video testimonials that moved me to tears originally going to http://www.theredwoodclinic.com/neurologic-relief-center-berkeley/)

Symptoms and Conditions Possibly Associated with

Meningeal Compression

Did I mention that the Central Nervous System (CNS) controls all of the functions in the body? And did you hear that the meninges, membranes that surround the brain and spinal cord can become compressed or torqued? This can cause decreased blood and oxygen flow that then results in neurological effects. The use of Neurologic Relief Center Technique (NRCT) can be beneficial if there is meningeal involvement.

What are the possible symptoms that points to the need for NRCT evaluation and treatment? These symptoms include:

- Chronic, widespread pain

- Painful hypersensitivity to pressure

- Tingling of skin

- Numbness

- Muscle spasms

- Weakness in the limbs

- Nerve pain

- Bowel problems

- Insomnia or sleep problems

- Cognitive disorders (called "fibro fog" or "brain fog")

- Difficulty in concentrating

- Memory problems

- Decreased attention and ability to multi-task

- Anxiety

- Depression

- Irritability

- Nervousness

- Chronic localized pain, including shoulder pain, neck pain, back pain, and hip pain

- Rashes

Other conditions that are common among patients who have meningeal compression include:

- Chronic pain of facial muscles

- Tingling, or "pins and needles" of the skin

- Fibromyalgia

- Irritable Bowel Syndrome

- Bladder and urination problems

- Skin disorders

- Headaches/Migraines

- Muscle spasms

- Hypoglycemia (low blood sugar)

- Rheumatoid arthritis

- Lupus

- Post-stroke symptoms

- MS

- RSD

Millions Suffer Chronic Pain of Fibromyalgia

As many as 18 million Americans suffer from fibromyalgia, a little-understood disorder that causes chronic, widespread pain and hypersensitivity to pressure. Its effects also go far beyond pain, to symptoms including fatigue, sleeplessness, difficulty in concentration, bowel and bladder problems and many others. For many, fibromyalgia syndrome can be debilitating. As pain is modulated and interpreted by the brain, maximizing brain health demands that we better understand fibromyalgia.

The name fibromyalgia comes from the Latin and Greek root words fibro- (fibrous tissues), myo- (muscle) and algos- (pain) – meaning muscle and connective tissue pain. The name is in fact a misnomer. Originally it described what was thought to be fibrous deposits in the muscles that caused pain. While it's true that some patients have muscle spasms so severe that they become fibrous, this has nothing to do with the cause of fibromyalgia.

In the past, fibromyalgia patients were often called hypochondriacs. Many times they were referred to psychiatrists, and it was not uncommon for sufferers to be institutionalized.

Only recently has fibromyalgia disorder gained recognition as a condition that deserves attention. In general, patients are receiving more respect today and are believed when they say they have a problem. But they may still be looked upon as drug addicts, or presumed to have a self-serving motive, when all they really need is someone to believe them and get them help.

Researchers estimate that fibromyalgia affects up to 6 percent of the population, with nine out of ten sufferers being women.

Medical practitioners don't know the cause of fibromyalgia, and while there has been an increasing amount of research over the past 30 years, there is little agreement on what fibromyalgia is and what to do about it. Aside from pressure tests – which themselves are disputed, there are no generally accepted, objective tests for fibromyalgia. In the end, most patients are diagnosed based on differentials – that is, a doctor reviews the history of symptoms and rules out better-known possibilities before determining that "fibromyalgia" is the best description.

Since the cause is unknown, there is no generally accepted treatment for fibromyalgia itself. Instead, doctors focus on relieving the symptoms, through a variety of medications, therapies and lifestyle changes.

Many doctors, in fact, question the existence of fibromyalgia as a distinct clinical entity. The failure of the medical profession to agree on the cause, treatment, or even existence of fibromyalgia has made it difficult for those suffering from the painful and debilitating symptoms to find answers.

The Neurologic Relief Centers takes a broader view of fibromyalgia; it believes fibromyalgia and other conditions are actually caused by compression of the meninges – the three-layered membranes that protect the central nervous system. The Center's team has created the Neurologic Relief Centers Technique ™ a treatment procedure for neurological disorders, including fibromyalgia symptoms. An initial Neurologic Relief Centers test may bring temporary relief and quickly determine if the long-term treatment will benefit the patient. I was selected to participate in the program in 2009 and have been trained in and working with appropriate patients since.

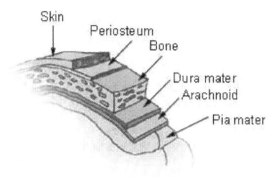

Meninges of the CNS

Meninges Form Vital Protective Sheath for Our Central Nervous System

The meninges are a three-part sheath of membranes that, along with the cerebrospinal fluid, cover and protect the central nervous system. The Neurological Relief Centers have developed a system of therapy based on the idea that compression of the meninges – Meningeal Compression – explains fibromyalgia and a myriad of neurologic diseases and conditions.

The outermost part, closest to the skull, is a thick, durable membrane called the dura mater. Its two layers form the outermost meningeal sac that covers the inner membranes and supports the larger blood vessels that carry blood from the brain back to the heart. The dura mater is attached to the skull and the bones that form the vertebral canal.

The middle membrane is called the arachnoid because of its spider-web structure. It serves to cushion the central nervous system.

The innermost membrane is the pia mater, a very thin, delicate envelope that is firmly attached to the surface of the brain and spinal cord. The space between the arachnoid and pia mater is filled with cerebrospinal fluid.

The meninges also contiguously surround the spinal cord and brain.

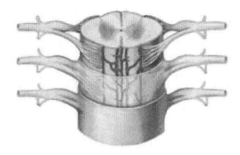

What is Neurologic Relief Center Technique?

The Neurologic Relief Centers Technique™ (NRCT) helps relieve the symptoms associated with neurological disorders such as Fibromyalgia, RSD (Reflex Sympathetic Dystrophy), Migraines, Chronic Fatigue Syndrome, Parkinson's Disease, Lyme Disease, Multiple Sclerosis and numbness and tingling of arms or legs.

The symptoms to these disorders can include headaches, migraines, chronic fatigue, digestive disturbances, sleeping difficulties, high blood pressure, brain fog, failed surgeries, body pain, facial pain, arthritis, nervousness, dizziness, breathing difficulties, wake up exhausted, communication problems, severe low back or hip pain and emotional difficulties.

So, what is Neurologic Relief Centers Technique™? (NRCT)

When you have had physical or emotional traumas (stress), tension can build up. The meninges surround the vertebral column, at the base of your skull and can pull on the meninges, which are not that flexible. Meninges are attached to all the nerve roots that exit your spine. When the meninges are pulled it could irritate those nerves.

NRC Technique (NRCT) releases the tension in the meninges thus releasing the irritation to the nerves.

When your nerves are irritated you may experience many symptoms because nerves control every function of your body.

A large number of health problems other than infectious diseases could be stress and neurological in nature. We advise everyone to be tested to see if NRCT (Neurologic Relief Centers Technique™) could help them.

NRCT is non-invasive and is usually painless. The doctor will perform a test to see how you respond to help determine if you are a candidate for NRCT. Many people respond to the test with a percentage of their symptoms relieved for minutes or days.

As of 2015, The Neurologic Relief Centers have over 200 offices throughout 6 countries.

But, some people don't know what these syndromes are. So this post will go over some of the syndromes and diseases that NRCT may be able to help.

Fibromyalgia

Because there is a lack of a specific test for fibromyalgia, diagnosing fibromyalgia has become more often a 'diagnosis of exclusion'—ruling out other conditions with a similar set of symptoms. Fibromyalgia tends to be treated rather dismissively, sometimes with cynical overtones. But the sufferers of fibromyalgia feel the pain, the sleeplessness, the fatigue, the depression, anxiety and stress.

The cause of fibromyalgia is unknown, but it is thought to be caused by long term stress—physical and/or emotional. The stress causes overactive nerve stimulation, which causes almost constant pain, which causes sleeplessness, which causes fatigue, which causes pain and on and on and on. There is no cure for fibromyalgia. Only reducing stress and controlling the symptoms.

RSD (Reflex Sympathetic Dystrophy)

Also called Regional Pain Syndrome, and like fibromyalgia, RSD can be difficult to diagnose and required excluding other conditions that produce similar symptoms.

RSD usually follows a physical trauma—a broken bone, an automobile injury—but not always. It starts with burning pain and swelling in the injured area and then spreads to the rest of the body. Sometimes symptoms can disappear for years and then reappear with another injury. Again, like fibromyalgia, there is no cure, only controlling the symptoms.

Migraines

Migraines are severe debilitating headaches that can last anywhere from 4 to 72 hours. There are many different reasons for migraines, from hormonal imbalances and diet, to environmental allergens and seasonal changes.

Migraines can be the result of a direct cause or be a symptom of another condition or syndrome. The severe headaches can be located anywhere in the head and can have the feeling of stabbing, throbbing or stinging. They can be accompanied with visions of flashes of light or tingling in the arms or legs.

Some people get migraines only once in their lifetime, while others have migraines several times a month.

Accompanying symptoms of migraines can include light sensitivity and nausea with or without vomiting.

CFS (Chronic Fatigue Syndrome)

The Centers for Disease Control (CDC) describes CFS as a distinct disorder with specific symptoms and physical signs, based on ruling out other possible causes. So like Fibromyalgia and RSD, CFS is 'diagnosis by exclusion.'

The exact cause of CFS is unknown, but may be caused by inflammation along the nervous system and that this inflammation may be some sort of immune response or process.

The most common symptoms of CFS are chronic and debilitation fatigue, muscle aches, joint pain and headaches. The symptoms can come on within a few hours or days and last for 6 months or more.

Parkinson's Disease

Parkinson's disease is a degenerative disorder of the central nervous system. It results from the death of dopamine-containing cells of the brain. The cause of cell-death is unknown. Early in the course of the disease, the most obvious symptoms are movement-related, including shaking, rigidity, slowness of movement and difficulty with walking and gait.

Later, cognitive and behavioral problems may arise, with dementia commonly occurring in the advanced stages of the disease. Other symptoms include sensory, sleep and emotional problems.

Lyme Disease

Lyme disease is an inflammatory disease spread through a tick bite that is infected with the bacterium Borrelia burgdorferi (B. burgdorferi).

The first symptoms resemble the flu and include chills, fever, headaches, fatigue and muscle pain. If treated with antibiotics at this stage further complications can be avoided.

If not treated, the symptoms of advanced stage Lyme disease include decreased concentration, memory disorders, nerve damage, numbness, pain, paralysis of the face muscle, sleep disorders and vision problems.

Multiple Sclerosis

Multiple Sclerosis is an inflammatory auto-immune disease that attacks and destroys the autonomic nervous system. The myelin sheath that covers the nerves is attacked and scarred.

Symptoms vary and episodes can last for days, weeks or months. These episodes alternate with periods of remission.

Because nerves in any part of the brain or spinal cord may be damaged, patients with multiple sclerosis can have many different symptoms in many different parts of the body. Symptoms can include loss of balance, muscle spasms, numbness, tingling, coordination problems, walking issues, tremors, weakness, constipation, urinary issues, vision issues, facial pain, decreased attention span, poor judgment, memory loss, reasoning difficulties, hearing loss, slurred speech, difficult chewing and swallowing to name a few.

There is no cure for multiple sclerosis.

This is a short list of the disorders and symptoms that NRCT may be able to help give relief. NRCT does not cure diseases and disorders; it just helps provide relief of the symptoms. And it has been successful.

If you or you know of someone who is suffering from any of these symptoms or disorders, it would be wise to contact a professional certified in NRCT for a relief test. The test is non-invasive.

Meningeal Compression and Fibromyalgia Pain

Meningeal Compression could be caused by an encroachment or twisting on the three-membrane protective covering of the spinal cord and brain, called the meninges.

This intrusion might be from a tumor or other malformation, but we find that it is most often caused by a change in the cervical spine, which can reduce or distort the space through which the spinal cord and meninges must pass.

Any tugging on the meninges can have devastating effects on this critical and sensitive nerve action, which in turn can produce a galaxy of undesirable symptoms.

We believe this compression creates myriad symptoms, one of which is fibromyalgia. Others are reflex sympathetic dystrophy (RSD), brachia neuralgia, trigeminal neuralgia, irritable bowel syndrome, restless leg syndrome, unexplained diffuse pain, depression, chronic fatigue, anxiety and many more.

The meninges are the three membranes that form a strong bag-like envelope around the brain and spinal cord, holds the cerebrospinal fluid, which brings nutrition and healing to the brain and spinal cord. It is attached to all of the nerves that pass through it.

Nerve roots are extensions of the spinal cord that turn and exit between each vertebra, sending and receiving impulses that control virtually the entire body, even the smallest parts. Since these nerves pass through the meninges, naturally it follows that every bodily system can be affected by the pulling of the meninges. These nerve roots also extend fibers to the brain, which transmit impulses that are then received as pain, burning, itching, hot, cold, tingling, or numbness, as well as other paresthesia (that is, odd feelings).

The pulling and irritation of these nerve roots cause nerve fibers to fire maverick impulses to the brain. The brain interprets these fired impulses as pain, itching, burning, coldness, numbness, or other odd feelings. The body, in response to stimuli from irritation, will often twitch or spasm, thus prompting the restless leg syndrome, muscle tightness, and spasms often experienced by fibromyalgia patients.

Typically irritation of the nerve roots, when it hits levels that are diagnosed as fibromyalgia, bombards the sufferer's brain, overwhelming the autonomic and sensory pathways, keeping them in pain, awake at night, fatigued, and depressed.

The symptoms of possible Meningeal Compression may vary from person to person. They may be debilitating - as in a severe case of RSD or Fibromyalgia - or be less severe in a milder case of fibromyalgia, mild facial pain or trigeminal neuralgia. Including the whole galaxy of symptoms would be impractical, because the nervous system controls the entire body and can affect all the systems. Here, then, is a partial list:

-       Insomnia: Insomnia is particularly troubling in almost all fibromyalgia patients. It could become worse in relation to the degree of pressure on the meninges. The anxiety, the pain, the overactive central nervous system, and adrenaline overproduction make sleep almost impossible.

-       Fatigue: Fatigue naturally goes along with insomnia, but it is a level of fatigue that goes well beyond what would be expected with ordinary insomnia, and it has a much deeper impact.

-       Emotional instability, depression, irritability, and nervousness: These symptoms are often the most difficult to deal with, since they affect the very core of the being and destroy joy and enthusiasm. Life becomes miserable for the sufferer as well as for those around him.

-       Mild to severe body pain: This can vary from headaches; pressure at the base of the skull; neck pain; arm pains or numbness; torso pain; hip, thigh, and leg pain; or numbness and facial pains. Often this will be worse in the morning and evening.

-       Headaches: Usually there is pressure at the base of the skull, and there is sometimes associated pain in the occipital (back side of the skull) and upper cervical spine (neck). Many patients have severe, migraine-type headaches. FMS headaches may vary in location and intensity. We have seen almost every possible combination—unilateral, bilateral, facial, occipital, mild, severe, —sometimes accompanied with nausea and vomiting.

-       Irritable Bowel Syndrome: This is present in most sufferers, and may be caused by the sympathetic nervous system firing constantly, preventing the parasympathetic nervous system from controlling digestion. Its constant firing may increase adrenaline production and bring with it a feeling of forthcoming destruction. The parasympathetic system works well when we are relaxed, and controls things like food digestion and normal, relaxed bodily functions.

- Rashes: Some people will develop rashes on their legs, arms, face, back, or other areas. Such rashes are common and almost always go away with the treatment.

- Trigeminal neuralgia: Observations suggest that the tugging on the trigeminal nerve as it exits through the meninges can trigger this symptom. Trigeminal neuralgia is characterized by facial pain, often lancing—usually severe, though it can be mild. The patients we have seen with this condition usually respond well to treatment.

- Calcium deposits under the skin: These are common, usually under pea size, but we have seen them much larger. They can be very painful and even cause bleeding with movement in rare cases.

- Communication problems: These are common. Symptoms of this sort generally suggest a severe case. Patients we see who are this ill are unable to answer questions or keep on the subject. This lack of focus usually abates in the first two weeks of treatment.

- Anxiety: Anxiety is often one of the most severe problems. Many patients don't even realize they have anxiety until it is pointed out. It can be brought on by the sympathetic nervous system firing continuously. It will push one, even though they may be totally exhausted, and keep them going somewhat; but it is this anxiety that also prevents sleep and rest. Panic attacks - feelings of a need to protect oneself or to run away - are common. When anxiety disappears, our patients become very tired and restorative sleep follows. This is when we see leaps in their improvement.

- All of the glands of the body can be affected, i.e.: the pituitary, the thyroid, the adrenals, the reproductive glands, the pancreas, etc. These glands malfunctioning can create a host of physical problems as well as mental and emotional problems. This is why balancing hormones give a person a boost.

- RSD or CRPS (Complex Regional Pain Syndrome): This is a complex and, until-now, misunderstood problem associated with an accident or a surgery. After the event the body part involved will continue to display pain and often circulatory problems. The pain can be excruciating.

The Neurologic Relief Centers Technique™ for Fibromyalgia Pain and Other Chronic Conditions

The Neurologic Relief Centers have developed a simple relief test that determines whether our complete treatment procedure will be effective for the patient who is suffering with severe chronic pain, fatigue, numbness, tingling, migraines, burning, but also symptoms associated with Rheumatoid Arthritis, Peripheral Neuropathy, Lupus, Multiple Sclerosis, TMJ, Fibromyalgia, Autism, High Blood Pressure, Insomnia, Failed Surgeries, RSD (Reflex Sympathetic Dystrophy), Trigeminal Neuralgia, Vertigo, Parkinson's and etc.

The relief that comes from the testing is usually profound and lasts from minutes to days. The test is not only diagnostic but also prognostic. Those whose symptoms are relieved by the test will almost always respond to treatment.

Like anything, the test is not perfect, but for those who have symptoms, it almost always brings relief in minutes.

The Neurologic Relief Centers do not claim to treat fibromyalgia pain and other neurological symptoms, just moving on the premise that it is a condition of the cervical spine causing an uncontrolled firing of the nervous system. The aim of our technique is simply to reduce the CSF pressure and/or meningeal compression that causes the symptoms of neurologic disorders.

The uncontrolled firing of the nervous system does not always come about from the same misalignment in every person. This results in different manifestations in different individuals, who understandably must be treated accordingly.

The procedure involves relieving the meningeal compression. It is a series of techniques that are applied at the appropriate times. Some of these are modifications of standard techniques and some we have developed.

The objective is to free up the neurological structures that are being encroached upon, thus allowing the brain and spinal cord to return to normal function. In most cases, there is little or no pain associated with this procedure. Where there has been severe trauma and many years in which to develop arthritis in the neck, the treatments may take days or weeks to bring relief.

The length of treatment for most people is generally three times a week over a period of eight to ten weeks (eight weeks usually works the best and is the standard for most patients), the treatment schedule often needs personal customization to meet individual conditions.

This is simply because it is in the nature of fibromyalgia and its causative mechanisms for the vertebrae to quickly return to the abnormal state where it has been for so long. And so it becomes of the utmost importance to hold the correction completely in place while the affected ligaments adjust and the body attempts to maintain this new position.

We have found that the longer the condition is present and the more severe the condition, the more intense the treatment needs to be.

Dos and Don'ts During and After Treatment

•Do not extend the head for more than a second or two.

•Do sleep with the head in about the same position as when you are standing.

•Do not sleep on your stomach.

•Do use a small pillow to support the head while lying on your back, but do not allow it to push against your neck. The pillow should go from your upper back to your head.

•Do, while lying on your side, put a pillow under your head, letting it support your neck, so your head is straight with your spine.

•Do not participate in activities that cause bouncing or jarring of the head for at least six months after treatment. We are trying to get the neck to stay in place. This condition is not like other neck problems and does not respond the same. It has been out of place for quite some time in most cases and will need all of the help it can get to stay there.

•Do not exercise other than walking during the first two months of treatment. Walk often but do not push yourself during this time. After the first month consult with your treating doctor concerning exercise. When you go home, the first six months are critical to help stabilization. Therefore the same rules apply. An exercise bike is good, or a bike that allows you to sit upright, or something that does not cause you to have to look up.

SUPER BRAIN: Maximize Your Brain Health for a Better Life

Post Care

Following the series of treatments with stabilization, one may need to have monthly or so treatments to counteracts the forces of day to day life. This might be as often as twice-monthly Stabilization Care treatments. Be sure and tell your Doctor if you have any returning symptoms. If you are travelling or move out of the area you will be assigned a Doctor in your area for Stabilization Care.

Irritable Bowel Syndrome

As many as one in five American adults may have the symptoms of irritable bowel syndrome (IBS), an often-debilitating condition that can cause abdominal pain or cramps, bloating, gas, and diarrhea and constipation. Twice as many women as men have the condition.

There is a high incidence of IBS among those who are diagnosed with fibromyalgia.

There is no certain cause for IBS, and diagnosis is generally a matter of ruling out other, better-known illnesses. Tests, such as colonoscopy, sigmoidoscopy or CT scans, are performed to eliminate other conditions, some of which could be life-threatening. Because the cause is unclear, treatment focuses on relieving symptoms.

One suspected cause is stress – and antidepressants, counseling and meditation are among the remedies sometimes suggested. The central nervous system is a focus, because the walls of the intestines move digesting food through the digestive system through a motion of contracting and relaxing muscles. An overly fast cycle results in diarrhea, a slow motion results in constipation.

Understanding the physiological processes involved in bowel function helps to determine what factors are involved. If dysbiosis or leaky gut syndrome are components, these are addressed by procedures such as the 4 (or5) R's system and with supplements for inflammation, digestive support, tight junction repair and support, and specific probiotics.

The Neurologic Relief Center technique has been helpful with many patients with IBS.

The NRC believes many symptoms may be explained by compression of the meninges – the three-membrane protective sheath of the spinal cord and brain - by encroachment or twisting. This may be caused by accidents, trauma and even stress.

The pulling and irritation of nerve roots cause nerve fibers to fire irregular impulses to the brain, the NRC says. The brain may interpret these fired impulses as pain, itching, burning, coldness, numbness, or other odd feelings. It may also affect the nerve impulses controlling the digestive system, causing the symptoms typical of irritable bowel syndrome.

A non-intrusive test can determine the suitability of the patient for long-term treatment with the Neurologic Relief Centers Technique™. The test also provides immediate temporary relief for many patients.

Sleep, Mood Disorders, and Chronic Fatigue

From 30 to 50 percent of adults experience insomnia or sleep disorders at some point, and an estimated 10 percent have chronic insomnia. The sleepless "epidemic" is reflected in the wide range of prescription and non-prescription sleep medicines and TV advertisements for cures.

A lack of sleep can be serious, leading to a lack of concentration, a higher rate of accidents, chronic fatigue and anxiety and mood disorders. Many of those suffering from fibromyalgia and other chronic pain disorders also suffer from lack of sleep or interrupted sleep.

While many things can cause insomnia – especially temporary bouts – one major cause is fibromyalgia and other chronic painful and debilitating conditions. The discomfort caused by the general pain, soft-tissue burning and tingling, and tender pressure points can interrupt or prevent restful sleep.

The Neurologic Relief Centers has developed a new approach to the understanding of the central nervous system that offers hope for a range of debilitating conditions.

The NRC says many such conditions are linked to Meningeal Compression, the encroachment or twisting of the three-membrane protective sheath of the spinal cord and brain, called the meninges. Most often, this is caused by an accident, trauma or stress.

"Any tugging on the meninges can have devastating effects on this critical and sensitive nerve action, which in turn can produce a galaxy of undesirable symptoms," says the NRC. Symptoms may include those diagnosed as fibromyalgia, reflex sympathetic dystrophy (RSD), irritable bowel syndrome, peripheral neuropathy, dystonia, restless leg syndrome, depression, chronic fatigue, anxiety and many more.

The pulling and irritation of these nerve roots cause nerve fibers to fire irregular impulses to the brain, the NRC says. These fired impulses are interpreted as pain, itching, burning, coldness, numbness, or other odd feelings. The body, in response to stimuli from irritation, will often twitch or spasm, sparking restless leg syndrome, muscle tightness, and spasms often experienced by fibromyalgia patients.

Further information on NRCT can be found here.
http://www.theredwoodclinic.com/neurologic-relief-center-berkeley/

CHAPTER 5: Feeding Your Brain. Does it Start in the Heart?

"The best and most beautiful things in the world cannot be seen or even touched, they must be felt with the heart." Helen Keller

As mentioned previously in the chapter on brain and nervous system development, the heart starts beating in the fetus around week six or later. That rhythmic vibration resonates throughout all of the developing cells in tandem with (but at a faster pace than) the heartbeat of the mother. There is bound to be some influence that that rhythm has – we all know how rhythms in music are something that gets us going. And the rhythms of rain on the roof can put us into a lulled sense of relaxation often. So feeding our brain through our heart beat is something that comes naturally through sound. But how else might the heart be feeding the brain?

Our quest to maximize brain health has other connections with our heart. Many people consider the heart to be a seat of emotion, particularly emotions related to love and relationships. At the same time we can certainly say that the brain is also an emotional organ, even though the "brainiac professor-side" of my personality may want to disregard the heart when thinking about optimizing brain health.

Of course, the brain needs circulation of blood and oxygen, so the heart's physical role in circulating blood is necessary. But the heart's role in maximizing brain health goes way beyond its pumping activity.

Your heart beats at various rates. Sometimes quickly, sometimes slowly. The way that the rhythm plays out over time varies. The pattern of this variation is called heart rate variability. A particular pattern of heart rate variability, a sine-wave coherent mode, was found in research as early as 1990 to cause higher brain waves to synchronize. This higher brain wave synchronization facilitated executive functions (of the neocortex) and higher cerebral cortex functions. It also helps people to improve their feelings, manage their emotions, and make clearer choices among other benefits. There are exercises one can do to achieve this, and there is a device that makes it easier to train oneself and then actually see and hear when you achieve the coherent heart rate variability. This machine has gone through a variety of upgrades over the years. I got one of the first models many years ago and have one that works on an iPad as well. Details of how to get this device can be found at http://www.theredwoodclinic.com/heart-rate-variability

What am I Grateful For?

I have had the great privilege to be able to do a lot of world travel in my lifetime. Of course, my travel was and continues to be as low-budget as possible. The experiences I have had travelling across the world have been incredible and invaluable to understanding other cultures and peoples. And even as a low-budget traveler, in many countries my low daily budget (we're talking $3 per day in the late 70s, food, shelter all together!) was more than what a typical local family of 5 or more might live on! I realized early on how much I had to be grateful for. The people in most of those countries would never have the same opportunities I had because they started at such a low income level and the exchange rates for their currencies were disadvantageous. For example, I would get 15 Nepalese rupees for 1 dollar (now it is closer to 50 rupees to the US dollar). In spite of this great good fortune, I sometimes forget to express gratitude. So I have to remind myself to remember (using my brain to find memories and things to focus on) the things I am grateful for and things/people/situations that make me happy and filled with love.

This practice of filling my heart with feelings of gratitude feels great and apparently it is also synching my brain through the amygdala to optimize my cognitive functions!! Win-win!

How to Use Your Heart to Synchronize Your Brain?

According to Deborah Rozman, PhD the following is the way that you help to synchronize your brain so that it has higher cognitive function and reduced bodily stress burden. "Focus on the area of your heart. You pretend that the breath is coming in through that area and out through that area, because that helps bring balance between the parasympathetic and the sympathetic nervous system. That helps set the stage to bring your autonomic nervous system into more balance. Then you activate a feeling of something you are grateful for in your life. The more you generally can feel that sincere feeling of gratitude or love, care for your pet, appreciation, or kindness, it's the feeling that creates that smooth wave form. That you can then sustain it without having to keep thinking about the breath, you end up feeling better, doing better, and that is the key to it; learning how to live more in the heart, in those positive heart feelings."

Feeding the Brain Through the Stomach

The heart is not the only organ that influences the brain. The digestive system has a significant influence as well. Particularly as that is the primary avenue that we use to get nutrients and natural medicinals into the body.

Key areas you need to address to maximize brain health include: reducing heavy metal toxicity in the body, balancing blood sugar levels, reducing inflammation anywhere and everywhere in the body, feeding your body with necessary nutrients like balanced amino acids, getting non-contaminated water in your body, getting your body's detoxification channels working optimally, and not putting things into your body that cause inflammation, sugar spikes, neurotoxicity, and imbalanced mineral content.

Avoiding Getting Neurotoxins in Your Body

As they say in the computer software industry, "GIGO – garbage in, garbage out." This applies to your body. Anything that goes in as food, liquid, supplements, medications, should be as low on the toxicity and allergenic potential list as possible.

Eat as organically as you can afford. Drink and cook with filtered water (http://www.multipureusa.com/redwoodclinic).

Boost Your Body's Cleansing Capacity

For removing heavy metals consider the following under professional supervision and monitoring:

Zeolite, Zinc, Andrographis, Tumeric (Curcuma longa) (Standardized), and Hops blend (Humulus lupulus)

For boosting your liver's detoxification capacity: UltraClear, AdvaClear, Silymarin, Alpha-Lipoic Acid, and others (http://www.theredwoodclinic.metagenics.com)

Some Ideas for Brain Enhancement from Different Angles

Herbal formulas containing: Folium Ginkgo Bilobae, Rhizoma Acori Gramine, Radix Polygalae Tenuifoliae, Radix Salvio Miltiorrhizae, Semen Biotae Orientalis, Poria, Tubor Ophiogoonis, Radix Rehmanniae, Semen Zizyphi Spinosae, Tuber Asparagi, Fructus Schisandrae, Radix Scrophularieae, Radicis Angelica Sinensis, Radix Platycodi Grandiflori, and Radix Ginseng

To improve brain blood circulation: ATP (Adenosine 5'-triphosphate), Xanthinol nicotinate, N-Acetyl L-Carnitine, Alpha-GPC (L-alpha glycerylphosphorylcholine), Vinpocetine, Huperazine A.

To improve the quality of the nerve cell membranes: DHA (docosahexaenoic acid), EPA (eicosapentaenoic acid), phosphatidylcholine, lecithin

There are various targeted supplements for neurotransmitter support that are best chosen based on careful analysis and individualized evaluation by a professional. They include: GABA: B-vitamins, (B6, B12) Magnesium, Zinc, Valerian Extract, Passion Flower extract, L-Theanine, Lithium orotate; Serotonin: Niacin, B6, Folate, B12, Magnesium citrate, St. John's Wort, 5-HTP, SAMe; Acetylcholine: Pantothenic Acid, Alpha GPC, N-Acetyle L-Carnitine; Dopamine: B6, L-seleomethionine, DL phenylalanine, N-Acetyl L-tyrosin, N-Acetyl L Cysteine, Beta phenylethylamine, Blueberry extract, Alpha Lipoic acid

Blood sugar support: UltraGlycemX, Glucogenics, ProglycoSP, cinnamon, chromium (http://www.theredwoodclinic.metagenics.com)

Addressing cofactors related to dementia: Proline-rich polypeptide complex, huperizine

The digestive system from the mouth to the anus has to be working properly to breakdown and absorb nutrients and to support immunological function, 70% of which is focused in the gut. A comprehensive evaluation of the GI tract is the best way to really optimize functioning of the digestive system for the purpose of supporting the brain. Even eliminating gluten and gluten related foods and substances can cause a significant improvement in brain functioning for many people. Functional medicine professionals can guide you on what tests and diets might work best to optimize your individual epigenetic needs. Learn more at http://www.TheRedwoodClinic.com

CHAPTER 6: Why Doctors Miss This (Why Doctors Forget Your Brain Function)

I have great respect and admiration for, and collegial relationships with many medical doctors. Physicians who have gone through the long and taxing medical school, internship, residency and licensing process to get a medical doctor's license. My Uncle Russ, an industrial medicine physician and skilled surgeon who I worked with side by side in the surgical suites of Indianapolis my summer after graduating from high school, was my role model. I have studied with a great number of MDs in my own career and learned so much from them. So this is the place I am coming from when I ask myself "Why do MDs largely ignore functional brain issues until they become more difficult to turn around?"

It is not from lack of basic neurological evaluation training, as that is part of general medicine practice. The details and subtleties of neurological breakdown is certainly known to most neurologists. I conclude that the specialization of medicine and the new insurance-oriented medical practice is the reason why so many brain degeneration and dysregulation problems are being overlooked or ignored. Medical insurance contracts are focused on symptom relief and rarely on cause correction because symptom relief is cheaper in the short run. Looking at the whole body and determining the levels that systems are functioning at takes time and money that just isn't paid for by insurance. And the main lab tests done, even in a "comprehensive blood panel" are evaluated based on how well the measurements fall outside of the really sick and pathological ranges but rarely for how well they conform to "optimal wellness values." The reference range is the 80th percentile; 80% of the population is overweight or obese!

But this insurance-based approach of the 2-4 minute clinical interaction misses a lot of areas that can be helped. It also eliminates the possibility of taking into account all of the factors I have mentioned previously, like toxicity, stress, meningeal compression, autonomic nervous system imbalance, hemispherical development imbalance, etc. It is not because these are irrelevant to health care and disease prevention – quite the contrary. Many people think that their insurance covers everything, or if the insurance doesn't cover it, it is not relevant. Again, bad approach.

A comprehensive approach is available but you have to value your health to have access to it. Professional athletes whose livelihood necessitates that they operate at peak performance (not necessarily at peak health) demand top dollar for their extraordinary abilities – but they also spend significant funds to get the evaluations and treatment they need to retain those abilities. How about you, Mr. or Mrs. Brain reading this sentence? Are you worth it to maintain or regain your top performance abilities?

How Often Should Your Brain Get Evaluated?

Get started today if you have never had a comprehensive evaluation. Then, after getting a thorough evaluation of your neurological, brain, and whole body functional status, your treatment plan and appropriate home work (stuff you do on your own) can be started. At a certain point as your functioning is improving and the indications of suboptimal functioning are looking better, you are ready to have follow-up on a routine basis. Experts like myself in this field of functional medicine agree that, depending on your circumstances, this may be on a monthly, quarterly, or semi-annual basis. Each person is different, but keeping up your neurological health is like keeping your house clean – doing it little by little on a steady basis makes for less severe situations cropping up and making it easier to keep things in great working order. Environmental influences are unpredictable and their impact can be mitigated by a step-by-step routine that helps support safety and comfort. Neglect is the mother of dysfunction. Further information available at http://www.TheRedwoodClinic.com/superbrain-faqs

CHAPTER 7: Dr. Jay's "B.R.A.I.N." Formula for Brain Health

To help busy people remember some key elements to maintaining a healthy brain (and memory), I have come up with my B.R.A.I.N. FORMULA. Each letter of the word "BRAIN" represents something that you have to think about and address in your life to successfully stay safe, sharp, alert, sexy, productive, and have an engaged life with family and friends.

- "B" stands for Blood Circulation.

- "R" stands for Remove toxins

- "A" stands for Avoid Sugar

- "I" stands for Inflammation

- "N" stands for Names

In this book and in _"Outsmarting the Dementia Epidemic: 7 Key Memory Care Factors to Avoid Alzheimer's and Successfully Keep Your Brain Safe, Sharp, and Sexy into the Future"_ I explore these 5 (it is 6 in Outsmarting!) elements of my BRAIN formula. I chose these 5 elements here because I feel that they will have the biggest positive impact on reversing the epidemic of dementia. There are many other elements to health and brain protection that can have an impact. The Alzheimer's Association and brain researchers at UCLA and elsewhere have stated that a multifaceted approach is necessary to address Alzheimer's. I wholly agree with this and do not think that there is a "silver bullet" discovery or drug that will change this trajectory.

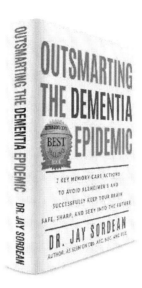

"B" STANDS FOR BLOOD CIRCULATION

What happens when blood and oxygen are cut off from your brain? A lack of blood or oxygen to any part of the brain for even a short time will result in malfunction and even permanent damage. A stroke is an example of this. This is why it is very important to take steps to keep your blood vessels open and filled with sufficient amounts of oxygen and high quality blood. How can you do that?

Acupuncture, NRCT (Neurologic Relief Center Technique), yoga, Tai Chi, other exercises, relaxation and meditation techniques, and certain natural supplements and herbs are necessary components of your health care routine to support healthy blood circulation as well as to undo negative influences of things like whiplash and blows to the side of the head.

My work as an acupuncturist, traditional naturopath, and NRCT practitioner has helped hundreds of patients with blood and oxygen deficiency and stagnation issues that were damaging their bodies and brains. Restoring proper function is a satisfying aspect of my work in helping others optimize their health. If you haven't done so already, watch the video explanation on how function is related to symptoms, stress, trauma, and toxicity at http://www.TheRedwoodClinic.com/symptoms-as-loss-of-function

Massage, shiatsu, chiropractic, osteopathic manipulation and various forms of exercise and meditation can increase the flow of blood to the brain by relaxing the muscles of the shoulders and neck as well. Blood to the brain is transported from the heart through the carotid and vertebral arteries. Tension in the neck and shoulder muscles causes decreased flow of blood through the vertebral artery. This was a discovery by Dr. Yoshiaki Omura during his research as a cardiologist. Thus, doing the above methods is a very important part of what any health care system should include. They are approaches I use in my own blend of help to support my own health and the health of patients.

"R" STANDS FOR REMOVE TOXINS

Many substances in the environment are neurotoxic. This means that they damage nerves and the brain which is composed of nerve cells. Well known neurotoxins include pesticides, volatile organic solvents, mercury, lead, aluminum, and cadmium. Clearing these chemicals and heavy metals out of our bodies is undeniably an important thing to do to reduce chances of memory loss, decreased brain ability and intelligence, tremors, Parkinson's, and other nasty degenerative conditions.

There are tests we can use to help elucidate toxicity and dysfunction of your liver, kidneys, and other routes of detoxification as well as foci of toxicity in your body. With that information we are able to support your body's ability to remove some of the toxic influences that will lead to damage of the brain and can lead to dementia. A detailed program for your particular situation is the best approach, but assuming that you do have toxicity in your body is a good bet. General supplementation that helps with detoxification support can be found online at http://www.theredwoodclinic.metagenics.com and other non-online sources we use to help patients.

"A" STANDS FOR AVOID SUGAR

Your body produces energy from sugar and your brain requires sugar to operate. However, that sugar (glucose) is produced internally and so we usually don't need that form of sugar in our diet directly. In other words, rarely do you need to put simple sugars in concentrated forms into your mouths to feed your body. You have heard of diabetes, right? Alzheimer's is classified as Type III diabetes. In other words, Alzheimer's is sugar-related. That is why it is being called Type III diabetes. High blood sugar also induces release of insulin and leptin, an appetite control substance.

Nutrition Tip: Starting the morning out with protein in your breakfast meal is known medically to buffer the shocks of sugar in the system and to reduce sugar craving.

Our stress-balancing program has helped many overweight people lose weight as a positive side effect. Our weight loss / healthy body composition program also reduces stress as a positive side effect. Go to our membership site to view videos on stress and on weight loss programs.

Hypoglycemia and hyperglycemia are two conditions related to blood sugar balance and imbalance. Fill out the surveys below to see if you might have either or both of these.

Enter the appropriate number - 0, 1, 2, or 3 - with 0 as least/never and 3 as most/always

___Crave sweets during the day

___Irritable if meals are missed

___Depend on coffee to keep going/get started

___Get light-headed if meals are missed

___Eating relieves fatigue

___Feel shaky, jittery, or have tremors

___Agitated, easily upset, nervous

___Poor memory /forgetful

___Blurred vision

___Fatigue after meals

___Eating sweets does not relieve cravings for sugar

___Must have sweets after meals

___Waist girth is equal to or larger than hip girth

__Frequent urination

__Increased thirst and appetite

__Difficulty losing weight

__TOTAL

If your total is 8 or more I suggest that you get evaluated more in depth. See Chapter 12

"I" STANDS FOR INFLAMMATION

Current research tells us that inflammation is one of the most significant factors related to decreased body function in general and brain degeneration specifically. Diabetes is also an inflammatory condition.

Long term diabetic patients have cognitive (thinking) disorders and memory difficulties. I have personally experienced what diabetes can do to the memories (and other parts of the body) in both clinical settings and personal experiences with relatives. Diabetes is not the only inflammatory condition that can occur in the body. Reducing diabetic tendencies and reducing inflammatory responses like gluten and other food sensitivities will help reduce the inflammatory factors that cause brain   degeneration.

For further information on how inflammation influences the functioning or your body, go to our membership sites and watch videos on gluten, inflammation, diabetes, SIBO (small intestine bacterial overgrowth), how to save your brain, etc.

Some of the supplements and medical foods that can help you address this inflammatory condition include ClearVite, UltraInflamX, UltraMeal360, a cinnamon product (MetaglycemX), all available online at http://www.TheRedwoodClinic.metagenics.com. Other supplements designed specifically for brain inflammation, poor blood circulation, and gluten sensitivity can be obtained by calling The Redwood Clinic to create a personalized program.   It is best to have a comprehensive functional medicine evaluation before starting to take these supplements and medical foods. *You can also get a special discount for certain products if you call the office before ordering online.*

"N" STANDS FOR NAMES

Next to public speaking, remembering people's names is something that adults often say they are not good at. It is time to change that way of thinking and practice. The way that we remember other people's names is by association. We associate a person's name (a sound and a series of written words or symbols) with a face, a voice sound, a feeling, a series of experiences, smells, emotions, and other things. Thus, practicing remembering names of people you have met helps your brain to access and use different parts of the brain. This improves brain flexibility of nerves (neuroplasticity) and helps to integrate different parts of the brain related to memory power.

Initial signs of dementia include forgetting names of pets. After you do our basic online brain assessment, we can fine tune areas of your brain that are showing signs of malfunction or non-optimal functioning and then create plans to potentially recover function if the condition is not too severe.

Complete our online survey to see if you are starting to have some indications or signs of memory loss. Send a copy of your receipt for this e-book to superbrain@gmail.com to get the online survey log-in details.

CHAPTER 8: Keys to a High-Performance Brain: Clearing Brain Fog & Enhancing Brain Capacity

"A person's psyche is at least as complicated as Indiana."
Steven Smith

Physiological Timelines

It takes 7 years to get a completely new body with respect to the actual chemicals that your body is made up of. It takes 7 years for the body to be completely rebuilt with "new" components. Your body actually is being rebuilt with "recycled" components as none of the elements (i.e. Carbon, Oxygen, Nitrogen, Hydrogen, etc.) are actually created anew from what we know of the conservation of energy and matter. So, you can be a new you over and over. So why not create a new energetic you as an overlay of the new chemical you?

It takes 90 days to totally change the red blood cells travelling through your body. Other cells have different life cycles. Change is constant and making the change count is how you optimize your life.

The basics of maximizing brain health are exercise, healthy diet, water, removing toxins, addressing negative memories and beliefs in the reptilian brain and cerebral cortex, learning to modulate stress responses, doing brain challenging activities, reducing the chances of developing dementia, protecting the head from injuries and concussions, and socializing with other people. The supplements and medical foods needed for supporting the body and brain were discussed in a previous Chapter.

Exercises and Practices to Tone-up and Calm Down the Brain and Nervous Systems

Some of the most effective exercises and practices for brain health work because it is a combination of movement, balance (Melillo's 6th sense), rhythmic breathing, and focusing your attention and awareness. They include Tai Chi Chuan, a Standing Zen exercise called "Ritsuzen," Yoga, and Chi Gong. Based on what was discussed ad nauseum in Chapter 2, you (the brain reading this) should understand why they work so well.

I have practiced various forms of Tai Chi and Chi Gong for over 40 years. I diligently practiced and taught Tai Chi Chuan for about 7 years, from age

18 to 25. This was concentrated and focused movement in a particular pattern, involving arms, hands, feet, legs, head, torso – all parts of the body shifting in all directions with balance changing. Circular hand motions, pushing forward, extending backwards, sliding out along the leg -- all of these motions of my hands coordinated with other body actions. And when doing acupuncture and shiatsu work with my hands, I focus attention on my fingers and palms of my hands to feel what is going on in the bodies in front of me. Thus, given years of this attention – awareness, my cold hands in the morning heat up quickly when using them in that deliberate fashion.

I have discovered that over the last 30 years I can do some subtle movements of my hands, or even just one hand, in a fashion like I would do Tai Chi. My whole body relaxes in the deals as if I have been doing 15 minutes of whole body Tai Chi! This happens in a matter of a few seconds. It is fascinating to me how this connection got created without my conscious intention. Small movements of one part of the body bringing out a whole body relaxation and awareness response. Do you remember the homunculus? There has to be a connection there, and perhaps the fact that I practiced diligently for 7 years.

At any rate, I suggest trying one of those exercise practices.

Working with Words, Music, Rhythm, and NLP to Change Dysfunctional Beliefs

I am a firm believer that our brain has patterns locked into it that help us run on autopilot. Many of those are hardwired and can't be changed. Others are soft wired and can be modified. Even the hardwired parts can be modulated due to relationships between the different hardwired components.

For example, the physiological stress reaction of your body is predictable and hardwired. However, how long it reacts and the degree to which it reacts are modifiable and are able to be controlled with practice. Alpha wave activity is a doorway to this control of the autonomic nervous system. The use of hypnosis, guided imagery, and declarations aid in our ability to reprogram our reactive stress patterns into responsive stress patterns. This is why I try to employ the use of particular hypnotherapy scripts into every acupuncture treatment done. Acupuncture works on the bodies electromagnetic control fields to reestablish appropriate dynamic equilibrium – tuning the autonomic nervous system to an alpha wave dominant state enhances the electromagnetic field benefits of acupuncture.

Of course, I utilize and promote the use of hypnotherapy outside the context of acupuncture as well. Helping people modify the internal dialogue/monologue scripts that run their behavior with hypnotherapy and guided imagery has huge benefits in improving brain health, productivity at work, and communication in relationships. Of course, all of these – work tasks, communicating, and emotional connections in relationships – are a function of the brain's activity. By maximizing your brain health you can optimize your life!

Declarations are positive statements made as if they are already accomplished. Like "I am rich, calm, and successful in all I do." Creating a series of these statements in a coherent way to direct and train your brain to have a positive internal monologue that supports your goals and dreams is another method to retrain your brain. This system helps build upon the way that your brain operates to direct all of our conscious and unconscious behavior. If there are behaviors and beliefs that don't serve us and others well, we can use declarations, practiced with spaced repetitions, to change the scripts that direct the behaviors we have that are the substance of the characters we play in our personal movie of life.

Approaches for Optimizing Brain Function and Addressing Functional Disconnection Syndrome

All of the methods I speak about in this book are applicable for optimizing and maximizing brain health. However, there are times that the brain has not developed in an even manner that it needs to for all functions to take hold. When that happens the condition may be classified as a Functional Disconnection Syndrome. It is thought that ADD, ADHD, Autism spectrum disorder and a variety of other neurological conditions can be classified as FDS. Just as there are many types of dementia. Dr. Robert Melillo and his colleagues have devised a system that has helped many people get the changes they are looking for, often by using specifically chosen unilateral activities to build weakness in aspects of the brain on one side. My chart of the two hemispheres' functions gives some insight into why this may be so.

Approaches Using Breathing for Brain Optimization

At this very moment I will beT that you are breathing, even if you are not aware of it. Breathing is a vital activity, without it we die. Using focused breathing techniques, like breathing into the lower abdomen and focusing attention of the breath entering and exiting out nostrils, are very effective to help change stress reactivity, reverse panic attacks, and improve the ability to think and do tests. Meditation practices, Dr. Ben's 3 legs of the stool for stress and test taking, synchronized heart and brain training through Heart Math – all use these principles. Even voice teachers instruct on breathing fully and only speaking when the abdomen is going in. I learned these while playing woodwind instruments in elementary and middle school and when practicing Tai Chi Chuan in college. Maximize brain health by breathing.

Learning Behavioral Systems Like BANK to Improve Human Communication and Reduce Stress

I have always been fascinated with learning new ways to better communicate with others. With dogs and cats you can just start petting them to establish rapport. Well, at least with most of them (the others—I urge exercising cautions to preserve your digits and calves). But with many people you can't just go up to them and start massaging their necks and playing with their ears.

There are many systems to better know how people operate so you can create better rapport. Remember, social interaction is a key element to brain health and balance. One that I employ with all new patients is the BANK card system. It is fun, engaging, non-threatening, and provides the other person with insights about themselves that helps them as much as me. This is an excellent communication and language building tool for your brain. Check it out and sign up for the in-depth training at the site I give you a complementary analysis worth $57!
http://www.playbankcode.com/drjaybankrapportcards

Dispelling the Hold that Certain Old Memories Have Over Our Life

Some events in our lives are burned deeply into our memory banks. They can rule our lives. Sometimes these are really helpful. Other times that are a major wall to living a fuller and happier life. Our brain has ways that can lock them in and ways to let them go. Some of the effective ways I have found clinically for patients include EMDR, somatic psychotherapy, rebirthing therapy, NLP techniques, hypnotherapy, declarations, and positivity stacking. Even negative beliefs about test taking can be addressed in a variety of ways listed above as well as the 3 legs of a stool system.

Playing Games is Intrinsic to the Human Brain for Happiness, Growth, and Creativity

Humans have invented I don't know how many games. Sports, cards, gambling, racing, how to get the guy, how to get the girl -- it goes on and on. Our brains are programmed to do games and to figure out puzzles, which is part of the game. Employing a variety of games in your life will help to your brain alive. This is known in the memory care communities and employed with great benefit. Make sure that you do a combination of team and individual games.

Strengthen the Neck to Protect the Head

It is known that many quarterbacks are injured with whiplash injuries that then throw off their timing, thinking, and alertness. Payton Manning had that happen to him and he worked very hard to get back his edge to restart his career. What isn't know well that those team hubs do not use what martial artists know, particularly those who sustain blows to their heads. It is vital to strengthen the neck muscles to help sustain the impact that does happen to the head when hit directly or with a whiplash effect from a body hit. It takes as much as two years of specific training to get sufficient stability of the head and neck to absorb the forces generated by those impacts.

Some Random Ways to Boost Your Brain Function

Enhance your brain resiliency and function by trying these on occasion: read a book upside down; watch a fish swim for 1 hour; write with your non-dominant hand (do this with written declarations to extra potency)

Detoxification Support Can't Be Emphasized Enough

Detoxification Regimens are important for everyone. To stay as healthy as possible you must remove toxins that are in your body and avoid putting more toxins into your body. Our bodies are more than 72% water. Removing toxins from the body is done primarily by making them more water soluble so that we can pee them out, poop them out, spit them out, sweat them out, and cry them out. The liver makes them more water soluble by a several step process. However, we want to prevent them from getting them into the body via water, food, air and skin contact. Thus, preventing toxins from getting into the body through our drinking water is a reason why everyone should use a water filtration system. Again, I highly recommend the Multipure system. http://www.multipureusa.com/redwoodclinic . The Multipure systems are easy to use, independently tested by Underwriters

Laboratory testing, easy to install, and have decades of reliability. I have used them in my home and at clinics since 1983.

You can also get information in video format online at the above website as well as by signing up for my video series on toxicity, water purification, and heavy metal toxicity testing at http://www.TheRedwoodClinic.com/Removing-Toxicity

How do we know if our body is clearing out heavy metals or other damaging chemicals properly and effectively? We can use modern laboratory testing that either detects the presence of the toxins, the presence of antibodies to the toxins, testing of your body's neurologic response to toxins, or testing the detoxification processes in your body and how competently they are removing the toxins. The pH of your saliva can be an initial simple test of toxic build-up in your body. That is one of the screening tests that we do onsite in our company wellness programs that corporations hire us to do for their wellness programs. Testing can be fairly generalized and less expensive and then be very specific and more expensive. But where health is concerned, what you spend to deal with toxicity in your body pays off big benefits in the future. Just think about the poisoning of Victor Yeshenko with a drop of DDT in his martini during the Ukrainian elections many years ago and the impact this can have on your life is more real.

But suffice it to say that there are tests we can use to help elucidate toxicity and dysfunction of your liver, kidneys, and other routes of detoxification as well as foci of toxicity in your body. With that information we are able to support your body's ability to remove some of the toxic influences that will lead to damage of the brain and can lead to dementia. A detailed program for your particular situation is the best approach, but assuming that you do have toxicity in your body is a good bet. General supplementation that helps with detoxification support can be found online at http://www.theredwoodclinic.metagenics.com and other non-online sources we use to help patients.

Smile Early and Often

One of my mentors is Clint Arthur. He suggests smiling until it hurts and then more so. Sales trainers tell us that smiling while making calls on the phone work more effectively because the person on the other end of the call can feel and sense that you are smiling. I think this is right as well. My daughter Elah told me that her dance teacher said that smiling tricks your brain into thinking it is happy. Can't argue with her dance teacher on this. And when you are working with a person with brain damage or dementia?

Smiling is always an effective way to make a connection. The brain some-how blossoms with a smile even when the rest of you is in the dumps. They also say that if a woman is depressed she should put on make-up in the morning and it will improve her mood for the day. Perhaps cosmetics are powdered or cream smile-juice.

"YES!"

I took a course on accelerated learning and Blair Singer was one of the teachers. A method that he had taught and which I have passed on to many others is the "YES" gesture.

The basic principle is that you think of a time when you were on top of the world. It was a big win for you. You felt confident, happy, a winner. You dwell on that, and when it is firmly fixed in your mind and you are feeling the positive feeling, you bend your arm, create a fist, and pump your elbow down saying "yes!" Just like many athletes and others do when they get something right. You practice this over and over and do it throughout the day. It will help you when your brain and energy is flagging.

When I want to "up my game" or get out of an emotional funk that is not serving me, I draw on my many great experiences and wins by pumping my arm, using the fist pulling-down gesture, and say "Yes! Yes! Yes!" It works every time. I also do it with the opposite arm to get a stronger effect and to balance my brain integration.

CHAPTER 9: Super Charge Your Child's Chances in Life

As a parent myself, I know how much the safety, happiness, and success of your child or children means to you. Life can be wildly wonderful and exhilarating. Life can be heart-wrenching, painful, and exhausting. And anywhere in between. Given the genetic and energetic connections that parents literally and inextricably have with their "offspring," no matter where your parent-child relationship lies currently, most parents want nothing but the best for their children, at least ideally.

The odds of this may be stacked in your child's favor or not due to circumstance. But improving the odds and chances cannot hurt. Based on my experience and training and the advice given by experts I interviewed, these are some things to enhance the brain capabilities of your children.

If you recall from my very lengthy discussion of "How the Brain Works," it all starts prior to conception. So all the recommendations I gave apply to you to begin with.

Then, during pregnancy, these are key:

- decreasing toxic exposures

- eat as organically as you can afford

- expressing and embodying gratitude

- taking the right vitamin mix, including pristine omega 3s with DHA content

- supplementing with probiotics

- creating a sound environment mixes with upbeat voices, music, and laughter

- communicating love with people around you

- massaging your belly gently in a clockwise motion

- taking care of your own brain and body function in a comprehensive way

After birth:
- continuing the prenatal routines

- doing my special energetic massage of your baby

- breast feeding your baby as long as possible, but at least 6-12 months

- consider delay of vaccinations until the immune system is more mature

- consider spreading vaccinations out so it is clear when and if a reaction occurs – further repeated vaccination with that substance is medically contraindicated by the manufacturer and FDA research should a reaction occur

- do not give your child anything that would suppress the reaction unless it is life-threatening; don't repeat that vaccination (so if you do all 8, or 10 or whatever at once, how do you know which to avoid next time?)

- give specific probiotics starting at about week 6 unless colic occurs sooner

- cradle your baby in such a way as to support a healthy posture into the future

- watch and reduce your own dietary intake and medication intake while nursing

- take your child in to an acupuncturist for Shonishin treatments (Japanese-style children's acupuncture)

- avoid antibiotics if possible – most earache pain is not bacterial – it is inflammation that can be managed in innocuous ways

- choose a hypoglycemic and low allergy potential diet

- exercise and get fresh air for you and your baby

- smile a lot

As the child passes through infant, toddler, and preschool stages:

- positive feedback from your heart

- don't overpraise, but boost self-esteem, especially if they have lung problems or asthma

- take your child for well-child and sick child visits to natural practitioners as well as the paediatrician

- encourage a wide range of play activities not involving the computer

- put your cell phone away when you are with your young child – interact with them and not the cell phone unless absolutely necessary.

- continue with the organic and toxicity recommendations

- have them take classes in Tai Chi, yoga, gymnastics, dance

- do games as a family that involve skill, remembering, patterns, laughing, watching facial clues (they may grow up to be poker players or interrogators!) and not video games—social interaction is key to brain health

- get periodic comprehensive child brain assessments at a competent facility

- do age appropriate trainings using the Keys from Chapter 8

- get meningeal compression evaluations

- get special help should you notice absent or sub-normal developmental milestones

- communicate your love verbally to your child with a smile on your face

Similar recommendations apply as they get older. The comprehensive functional evaluations I do at my office become appropriate for ongoing monitoring of brain and body health for the life of an individual from about age 4 onward due to the nature of the survey forms. Prior to age 4 we use other ways to evaluate if there is a brain imbalance going on. These ongoing and periodic evaluations are especially important if the child is engaged in contact sports or has accidents that involve the head, neck, spine or other parts of the body connected to them.

In summary, as all of the professional clinicians I interviewed about this said, first off you have to protect the brain, which is very important; you have to exercise the brain and your body; and you have to nourish the brain. All three are needed ensure the future brain health and neurological health of your children.

CHAPTER 10: Life as Independent Living Versus Memory Care

No one can predict where the twists and turns of life will lead them as they age. Early on there could be debilitating accidents or conditions that forever change the course of later life. Christopher Reeve lived with paralysis for years. Stephen Hawkins has been confined to a wheel chair and the use of a computerized voice doing his speaking for his brain. Some people die in their 100s lucid and needing only assistance in certain tasks – others have progressive Alzheimer's requiring constant care either by family members or in a memory care community.

While we can't predict where our life will lead us, we can take many steps now to increase the probability and chances that our brain will be as healthy as possible. Of course, that is the purpose of this book.

If we do end up needing special care, what are the options we can look forward to other than, or in addition to, family and friends taking care of us?

Barring a situation that puts us in intensive nursing care or on life-support, being mobile and somewhat able to move our body around, for some the thought of aging into serious dementia is not a choice we would want to make consciously. But, many of us are doing just that by our choices now. What could that turn out to be like?

As a reminder (to the brain reading this book, YOUR brain), Alzheimer's is one of the many forms of dementia. Dementia is a condition where cognition (ability to think) and memory are weakened. There are many known risk factors and conditions that effect memory strength.

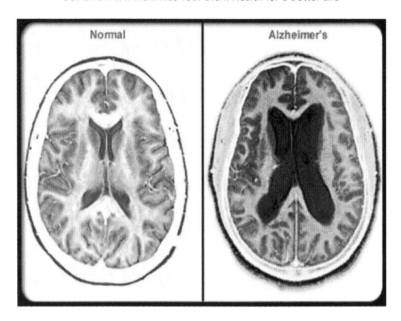

I have interrviewed many people for this book as well as thousands of patients over decades. A representative story of Alzheimer's goes something like this, as described by a woman who is a professional in the field of aging and memory care placement.

A Story of Grandma with Alzheimer's

"We took care of my grandmother with Alzheimer's. Grandma lived in a mobile home by herself for many years. We grandchildren would go and visit her from time to time. Her own daughter, my mother, was estranged from Grandma. At one visit to grandma, we found her alone in her mobile home with only a jar of peanut butter to her name. Grandma wasn't able to take care of her own basic needs because of brain degeneration. Initially, I – as her granddaughter - dropped in on Grandma, and then someone had to leave work and become a full time caregiver. Other family members couldn't help give Grandma money to live on because they themselves had high medical costs and needs. Thus, her daughter (my mom) and I (the granddaughter) had to eventually also pay for Grandma's board and care. They both had to work to survive and there was no money to pay for a home care person to come to take care of Grandma."

"So Grandma was put in a board and care facility. It was bare bones – no special activities to help keep up Grandma's mental and physical functioning. Just a T.V. that she and others would sit in front of hours on end. Certainly there was no blame on the part of the board and card facility – they were operating on a shoestring budget as well. I and my mother would come by and take Grandma out for various activities until she eventually passed on after years of this level of living during the last days of her life."

Levels and Types of Care Facilities

Care of loved ones and family members as they become older and are less able to care for themselves is set up in a graduated system of different types of facilities. Each facility or community is set up and organized based on the amount of care that is needed or desired.

At the leanest level are what has become known as "hospitality care" facilities. They are "like a cruise ship," making your life easier by providing a place to live and providing food services. This is all some people need to make their lives easier as they are starting to lose the "independence" and "freedom" functioning they used to be able to provide for themselves.

The next level up is a place where further assistance is needed. This could be laundry and bathing care. At this level it becomes "assisted living." This type of facility is where licensing comes into play, and the cost goes up because professionals have to be brought in to provide the added services.

The next step in the "living assistance system continuum" is skilled nursing. A medical presence is required all the time. These communities are very expensive but provide an environment of complete acceptance and understanding of the needs of the residents. They take a huge burden, physically and psychologically, off of the surviving family members and spouses. Each higher level of care often incorporates various levels underneath them. However, there are also assisted living and skilled nursing facilities without independent living units. There are also memory care communities that are nothing but memory care – or taking care of dementia and Alzheimer's patients, also know as "forgetfulness care."

The sizes of facilities varies, but the number of residents, or community members, can be from 4-8 to as many as 250 in the larger organizations. Some of the larger organizations can have a mix of independent living, assisted living, skilled nursing, and memory care units.

The memory care units are the highest level of control of residents. Memory care is geared for those with dementia and Alzheimer's. Residents are monitored carefully and in "locked in" status because their memory is so deteriorated that they cannot remember where they are or how to get back on their own even if they are allowed to leave. It is not safe for the residents nor for the facility that is responsible for the care of the resident. Nevertheless, sometimes a resident will wander away in spite of the best intentions of the staff. Allowing them to come and go at will is not possible. These communities are very expensive but provide an environment of complete acceptance and understanding of the needs of the residents. They take a huge burden, physically and psychologically off of the surviving family members and spouses.

The cost of these different care levels ranges widely. For the simple "hospititality care" in a 4-8 unit facility the service costs (in California) can be from $750 per month on up.

Memory care facilities are in the $5000 and greater range per month. This is taking into account the possibility that residents have Medicare or other medical insurance coverage, social security or pension payments, or long-term care insurance benefits. Still, although the high monthly cost is totally justified by the cost of running the facility with trained professionals caring for the residents / community members, the financial impacts of needing this level of care is overwhelming for so many families or individuals unless they are quite wealthy.

More can be learned about the range of facilities available, how they operate, and the deep caring that the professionals who work there have for the residents by listening to my podcast and reading my blog at www.TheRedwoodClinic.com.

Taking Care of Your Brain Now May Be the Best Alternative

Avoiding this possibility or at least decreasing the time required to live in such a circumstance is the most reasonable approach. I hope that my detailing, here in this chapter, the system of care for people in declining brain (and body) functioning motivates you, the reader, to make some changes now when it is hopefully less expensive.

The largest cause of bankruptcy in the U.S. is said to be due to medical bills. The high cost of medical insurance and care in the US is said to be due to spending 80% of health care dollars on the last few years of life. The personal quality of life and the societal quality of economic viability both turn on how well one takes responsibility for one's own brain care. Enhancing brain health can indeed lead to a better life.

CHAPTER 11: Caveat at end of Super Brain

"You come into this world with nothing. You leave this world with nothing. All you have left is what you give when you're here." Wayne Dyer

"Pride is the most expensive thing you own. Your reputation is the most valuable thing you own." Dr. Gaelen Graham.

Not to be Read by the Faint at Heart (I'm Not Sure if Even *I* Understand What I Wrote!)

At a certain point in my high school years of mathematical study I learned that division by zero, in other words, x/0, was undefined. I thought that odd, and from then until now I have had in the back of my mind a motivation to define it. I spent time writing thoughts on this definition while I lived in Japan as a graduate student, drawing some pictures to represent what I thought that x/0 meant.

A mathematician in Berkeley, California who I met in the first years after I moved from Philadelphia, told me that it was not really that it was undefined; it was just that it couldn't be solved when using the usual rules of mathematics and relative to base ten math. (The math that we use most often in common calculations, with 10 digits to choose from and using a "place" system of "one's," "tens," "hundreds," "thousands," etc.)

As I further pursued my understanding, or at least trying to understand what other smarter people were saying about physical reality, I came upon, and was kindly given books on string theory, holographic paradigm, etc. These became the basis for my further exploration of "how things work," how memory works, what thought is. You know, light stuff.

A recent article in Scientific American, August 2013, by Meinard Kuhlmann titled "Quantum Physics: What is Real" therefore caught my attention serendipitously as I was going to read an article about "How Sleep Shapes Memory: Shut-eye prunes the day's chaff and restores neural balance." So, what does this article about reality have to do with this book and its contents?

Throughout this book I have talked about what is the substance of our experience as humans. How our brains and bodies develop, what has to be there to create the highest level of our functioning from the standpoint of what we know about the brain and other body parts. This is all based on the assumption that 4 dimensional reality is largely what our lives are about. Living in space (three dimensions) and through time (birth, life, and eventual death). Time is considered the fourth dimension from a western and scientific perspective. So, 3 dimensions plus 1 dimension equals 4 dimensions. Our 5 senses studied by physicians are considered to be a function of 4 dimensions.

However, those people who study the physical realm, physicists, have gotten to a point of studying both the macrocosm (the planets, stars, universe, etc.) and the microcosm (subatomic particles and properties) that what is "real" is not just 4 dimensional reality. It is way beyond 4. And thought is such a strong influence on how "physical things" behave and what is considered to be "physical things," we come to a place that you are fully justified in questioning everything I have said in this book so far!

For example, are thoughts a function of the brain alone? Again, since high school and my desire to define division by zero, I also created a postulate (or quasi-self-evident truth) that thought is faster than the speed of light. This is in spite of the rule in physics that nothing is faster than the speed of light.

Are you following what I am saying? To reiterate, the CAVEAT is as follows. I have spoken here of a variety of things, processes, actions, matter and phenomenon as being "how things work." Putting our attention also on the brain and spinal cord assumes that they are material, in space and time. And they are in the location where all this thinking, feeling, sensing and remembering occurs. The fact that we can hold our brain in our hands (at least metaphorically) and sense it (feel, see, hear, taste, smell) lends credence to our belief that it exists. And what of thoughts? Do they exist?

Thoughts can represent real things, but the thought itself is not a physical thing we can hold or sense. Physicists studying "how things work" and physical reality have laid out theories that work to enable us to create things that move and stop predictably. Like cars, planes, etc. On the other hand, physicists, according to Meinard Kuhlmann, have come to the point that the fundamental ideas and theories about building blocks of atoms, (the atoms that are the building blocks of the chemicals that we talked about in brain function with neurotransmitters) cannot even be comprehended by most physicists themselves. Physicists can measure things but they can't say what the objects really are. Nor can they say where the object is located (as a subatomic level). So we exist somewhere at the atomic level but not at the subatomic level.

We can also note that damage to our brain tissue alters the way that we operate as individuals – if the damage is not severe, we notice the changes in our behavior as do others. If it is very severe others note a change in our behavior and yet perhaps we are not aware of our own change in behavior because maybe we can't perceive in the same way because our sensory apparatus has changed.

So, I discussed our life and existence as a function of the brain. I stated that your brain is the focus of your life, personality, your experiences. My title suggests that creating a super brain, by maximizing brain health, will lead to a better life. This all presupposes that thoughts are a function of your brain. If thoughts are not only in the 4-dimensional (corporeal) reality, and are not simply a product of your brain, then much of this book can be taken with a grain of "caveat" salt.

I would like to conclude with a quote by Albert Einstein

The human being is a part of a whole called by us universe, a part limited in time and space. He experiences himself, his thoughts and feelings as something separated from the rest, a kind of optical delusion of his consciousness. This delusion is a kind of prison for us, restricting us to our personal desires and affection for a few persons nearest to us. Our task must be to free ourselves from this prison by widening our circle of compassion to embrace all living creatures and the whole of nature in its beauty.

CHAPTER 12: RESOURCES

ABOUT THE AUTHOR

Dr. Jay Sordean is an author, speaker, cable TV program producer, a licensed acupuncturist (L.Ac.), Oriental medical doctor (O.M.D.), certified traditional naturopath (C.T.N.), Qualified Medical Evaluator (Q.M.E.), homeopath, and herbalist. He is fluent in Japanese and has been in the clinical practice of natural care for over 30 years.

Patients find that Dr. Sordean's warmth, sensitivity, and experience are valuable assets to help meet their individual needs, whether in treating acute illness, chronic disease, work or personal injury, infant and pediatric conditions, or for life-long brain health promotion and disease prevention. Patients also appreciate his ability to communicate effectively with other physicians and his dedication to advocate a holistic and preventative approach treatment. As one patient recently stated, he is "more than just a doctor." –S.N.

Dr. Jay Sordean is a popular and sought-after speaker on the topic of "Saving your Brain and Memory" before many audiences since 2007. Many of these lectures are recorded and posted on YouTube under The Redwood Clinic and were broadcast on Berkeley public access cable television in the series "Natural Solutions with Dr. Jay".

In 1971, following the death of his father to lung cancer metastasizing to the brain, Dr. Sordean began his focus on Oriental Medical studies with the practice of Tai Qi Chuan, Shiatsu, and dedicated study of Japanese. His formal training in acupuncture and herbology began in 1973 during his first trip to Japan and has continued thereafter with study in Taiwan, Hong Kong, Japan, and other areas of Asia, Europe, the United States, and Canada. His training in homeopathy began in the late 70's and includes residential clinical study in Calcutta, India and Practitioner of Classical Homeopathy status from the Dynamis School for Advanced Homeopathic Studies in England.

In 2005, Dr. Sordean achieved Medical Provider Certification in the First Line Therapy program to put patients on the path to optimal health and ideal body composition through a combination of balanced eating, exercise, reduction of stress, appropriate testing, and effective supplementation. He also has specialty training in pediatrics, immunology, orthopedic and neurological acupuncture.

In 2009, Dr. Sordean was trained in the new Neurologic Center Relief Technique. This new needleless technique can help people with seizures, Parkinson's, dementia, fibromyalgia, rheumatoid arthritis, mental "fog," RSD, insomnia, anxiety, digestive trouble, chronic migraines, and other chronic pains. Dr. Sordean is nationally certified by the National Commission for the Certification of Acupuncturists as a Diplomate and a Diplomate of the National Board of Acupuncture Orthopedics. Less than 1% of the acupuncturists have achieved his level of advanced training.

Recommended by the Author

Alzheimer's Association: A source about Alzheimer's and local and national resources and events related to Alzheimer's and dementia for caregivers. www.alz.org

Resources on the first five years of life for children's development. (Just make sure that you do it organically and with filtered water) http://www.ccfc.ca.gov/parents/learning -center.aspx?id=9

The Redwood Clinic

3021 Telegraph Avenue, Suite C, Berkeley, CA 94705:

A natural medicine clinic with expertise in evaluation and natural treatment of neurological, brain and other health issues from a wholistic perspective.

CALL TODAY:
+1-510-849-1176

For a free brief online brain assessment
& to sign-up for a Free Video Education Course
on "How to Protect Your Brain"
www.TheRedwoodClinic.com/Removing-toxicity

DISCLAIMER: The information written in this book is designed to provide helpful information on Alzheimer's, memory, and the subjects discussed. It is not comprehensive by any means. The book is not meant to diagnose or treat any medical condition, or to replace the advice of your physician(s). The author of this book does not claim to have found a cure for Alzheimer's or any other specific condition.

The reader should regularly consult a physician in matters related to his or her health, particularly with respect to any symptoms that may require diagnosis or medical attention. For diagnosis or treatment of any medical problem, consult your own physician(s).

The publisher and authors are not responsible or liable for any damages or negative consequences from any treatment, action, application or preparation to any person reading or following the information in this book. References are provide for informational purposes only and do not constitute endorsement of any websites or other sources. Readers should be aware that the websites and contact information listed in this book may change.

DISCLOSURE: Some of the links are to places that you can purchase products that I recommend. The author or The Redwood Clinic may receive compensation or fees for the purchases – that covers the costs of business and publication expenses and in no way diminishes the value of the suggestions or recommendations.

Made in the USA
San Bernardino, CA
10 November 2015